BASIC economics

Butterworths BASIC Series includes the following titles:

BASIC aerodynamics
BASIC economics
BASIC hydraulics
BASIC hydrology
BASIC investment appraisal
BASIC materials studies
BASIC matrix methods
BASIC mechanical vibrations
BASIC molecular spectroscopy
BASIC numerical mathematics
BASIC soil mechanics
BASIC statistics
BASIC stress analysis
BASIC thermodynamics and heat transfer

To our parents

BASIC economics

Chris Brownless
Principal Lecturer, Department of Economics
North Staffordshire Polytechnic
Stoke-on-Trent

Stephen Hurd
Senior Lecturer, Department of Economics
North Staffordshire Polytechnic
Stoke-on-Trent

Ken Randall
Principal Lecturer, Department of Economics
North Staffordshire Polytechnic
Stoke-on-Trent

Butterworths
London . Boston . Durban . Singapore . Sydney . Toronto . Wellington

First published 1985

© Butterworth & Co. (Publishers) Ltd. 1985

British Library Cataloguing in Publication Data

Brownless, C.
   BASIC economics. – (Butterworths BASIC series)
   1. Economics – Data processing   2. BASIC
   (computer program language)
   I. Title   II. Hurd, S.   III. Randall, K.
   330′.028′5424   HB143.5

ISBN 0-408-01569-1

Library of Congress Cataloging in Publication Data

Brownless, C. (Chris)
   BASIC economics.

   (Butterworths BASIC series)
   Includes bibliographies and index
   1. Economics.   2. BASIC (Computer program
   language)   3. Economics – Research – Data processing.
   I. Hurd, S. (Stephen)   II. Randall, K. (Ken)
   III. Title. IV. Series.
   HB171.B765 1985   330′.028′5424   85-11299
ISBN 0-408-01569-1

Photoset by Butterworths Litho Preparation Department
Printed and bound in England by Page Bros (Norwich) Ltd, Norfolk

Preface

This book introduces students to the design of relatively simple economic models in BASIC. Many of the programs and exercises have been used as workshop activities with first year undergraduate students, but they can clearly be used with students on a variety of economics courses from A-level upwards.

The programs have been written using a small subset of BASIC, which is common to most micro and mainframe computers. Minor modifications will inevitably be required for certain computers, and in such cases it will be necessary to consult the relevant computer manual. Two of the programs make use of an optional graphics routine listed in the appendix to the book. Versions of the routine are given for the BBC, Apple II and RML 380Z/480Z microcomputers.

There is a progression through the book from short and simple to rather longer and more complex programs and economic applications. Chapter 1 introduces the main BASIC commands, assuming no previous knowledge of programming. It also serves as a reference source on BASIC. Chapter 2 builds up confidence in the use of BASIC by building up programs in simple stages. In succeeding chapters programs are presented which demonstrate clearly the differences between comparative static and dynamic analysis.

We wish to thank colleagues and students in the Department of Economics at North Staffordshire Polytechnic who have tested programs and exercises, and particularly Alan Greenwood and Richard Ledward for their valuable advice.

CJB
SJH
KVR
1985

Contents

Contents

Chapter 1

Introducing BASIC

1.1 What is BASIC?

BASIC is the language used in most educational uses of computers, and is designed so that you can start using it immediately. You control the computer by giving it *commands* and telling it to *run programs*.

1.2 Getting started

Starting the machine: on microcomputers you switch ON, on terminal systems you have to make sure you are connected to the main computer. If you are unsure about your system, ask the relevant computer expert.

Getting into BASIC: on many microcomputers you are straight into using BASIC as soon as you switch on. In other systems you have to give commands to load:

1. The operating system (which runs the computer)
2. BASIC (which translates your program into machine-readable code)

If you are using a terminal system, this stage may involve giving some form of *password*.

Once you are using BASIC you can write a program.

1.3 Programs

A program is a series of instructions written in a computer language such as BASIC. Once written it can be SAVEd and used over and over again.

1.4 A simple program

The following program calculates how much someone will spend on food.

```
210 PRINT"Demand for Food"
220 PRINT
230 PRINT"Income (in pounds) please"
240 INPUT Y
310 F=0.25 * Y
510 PRINT
520 PRINT"At an income of ";Y
530 PRINT"spending on food is ";F
540 PRINT
```

If you type it in, pressing the RETURN or ENTER key at the end of each line, you can then type LIST.

The LIST command gives a line-by-line listing of the program currently in the computer's memory.

It should look exactly like the example above. If it does not, you can change any line by retyping it. The computer automatically replaces the old line if you type another with the same number.

If you type RUN the computer will carry out the program in line number order. You will see something like this on the screen:

```
>RUN
Demand for Food

Income (in pounds) please
?6000

At an income of 6000
spending on food is 1500
```

(I am assuming you typed RUN and 6000).

You will see that the program really consists of three kinds of lines:

PRINTing, INPUTing and CALCULATING

and we now deal with each of these in turn.

1.5 PRINTing, INPUTing and calculating

Lines with PRINT at the beginning are used to output information to the user. In this case the output is sent to the screen, we shall see later how it can be sent to a printer.

There are 3 main uses of PRINT:

1. PRINT "text" – prints what is in quotes
2. PRINT F   – prints the value of the variable F
3. PRINT   – prints a blank line

Lines with INPUT at the beginning are used to accept data from the keyboard. So INPUT Y means that the user will supply the value for the variable Y for use later in the program.

A line: F = Y ∗ 0.25 means:

take the number 0.25
multiply it by the value of variable Y
the result is the new value of variable F

So the line is really *assigning* a value to a variable. So we can have a line: F = F + 1 which is not nonsense. It means add 1 to the value of F.

BASIC arithmetic has some peculiarities.

Plus and minus are conventional: + and −, but multiply is ∗, and divide is /.

↑ means raise to a power, A ↑ 2 is A squared.

Brackets are used conventionally, but only round brackets () are used.

If you are in any doubt about how a formula would be calculated break it up into several small steps, each on a separate line of the program.

1.6 Program planning

It is always sensible to have a structure to a program. One possibility is to write all your programs using a framework or skeleton such as:

```
LINES      1 -  89   A DESCRIPTION of the program
          90 -  99   Set DIMensions of ARRAYs
         100 - 199   Set the INITIAL VALUES of variables
         200 - 299   INPUT data for the program
         300 - 499   Do the CALCULATIONS necessary
         500 - 899   OUTPUT the results
         900 - 989   An option to RE-RUN the program
         990 - 999   END OF PROGRAM message
        1000-        for SUBROUTINES and STORED DATA
```

and you can make the structure clearer by putting in REM lines:

```
10    REM *****************************
20    REM * Name      What program does  *
30    REM *            (continued)        *
40    REM *            To run on :        *
50    REM * Version no:    Dated:         *
60    REM * Author(s) :                   *
70    REM *                               *
80    REM *****************************
88    REM
89    REM *** DIMENSION ARRAYS HERE ****
98    REM
99    REM *** SET INITIAL VALUES HERE **
198   REM
199   REM *** INPUT VALUES HERE ********
298   REM
299   REM *** CALCULATIONS START HERE **
```

```
498   REM
499   REM *** OUTPUT OF RESULTS HERE ***
898   REM
899   REM *** OPTION TO RE-RUN PROGRAM *
900   PRINT
910   PRINT "Type 1 to End the Program"
920   PRINT "     2 to RUN it again"
930   PRINT
940   INPUT Q9
950   IF Q9 = 1 THEN 990
960   IF Q9 = 2 THEN 100
970   PRINT "Please type 1 or 2"
980   GOTO 910
988   REM
989   REM *** END OF PROGRAM MESSAGE ***
990   PRINT
995   PRINT "End of Program"
998   END
999   REM *** SUBROUTINES START HERE ***
2998  REM
2999  REM *** STORED DATA STARTS HERE **
```

We use this general framework for some of the simple programs in this book.

You will notice three new types of line in this program:

REM, GOTO and IF . . . THEN and we now explain what they do.

1.7 Remarks

A line which begins with REM (which is short for REMark) adds comments to the program, for instance giving 'internal documentation' of the program as in lines 20–90 above.

REM lines are purely for our information, and are ignored by the computer when it carries out the program. So it is no use explaining your intentions in a REM line and expecting that to make up for your deficiencies as a programmer!

1.8 Jumps (GOTO and IF . . . THEN GOTO)

Normally the program is carried out in line order. So if we want the computer to jump over a section or go back to a previous section we use jumps.

We see the two simplest ways of doing this in our skeleton program in section 1.6.

GOTO jumps to the specified line number
(whenever it gets to the line 980 the computer goes to line 910)

IF . . . THEN GOTO This jump only takes place if the statement after IF is true. For instance:

at line 950 we check if Q9 is 1,
if it IS we jump to 990 and end the program.
(We asked the user to INPUT 1 to end the program or 2 to carry
on)
if Q9 is *not* 1 we carry on to line 960 as usual.
at line 960 we check if Q9 is 2,
if it IS jump to 100 and start the program again.
if Q9 is *not* 2 carry on to the next line.

IF . . . THEN GOTO has to be written in full on some machines
(such as Sinclair). On *most* machines it can be shortened to IF . . .
THEN, on some to IF . . . GOTO. If in doubt use the full version.

1.9 A branching program

Logically we can think of IF . . . THEN as being a *branch* in a
program. For instance we may know that households with children
spend a higher percentage of their income on food.

So we can add some lines to our Food Demand program from
section 1.4:

250 PRINT "Number of children in household"
260 INPUT C

and branch according to the value of C

305 IF C > 0 then 330
330 F = 0.29 * Y

assuming that households with children spend 29% of their income
on food, as opposed to the 25% spent by other households.

We then have to ensure that when the childless households have
had their spending calculated at 25% at line 310 it is not changed
to 29% at line 330, so we insert:

320 GOTO 510

which jumps over the calculation at line 330.

So we have two kinds of branches, those which check conditions
(IF . . . THEN), and those which *always* jump over a section of
program (GOTO). In computer jargon they are often referred to
as *conditional* and *unconditional* jumps.

1.10 Flowcharts

One problem in understanding programs is that they are written as
one sequence of lines whereas they really have lots of branches.

One way round this is to make a diagram of the structure called a flowchart. As an example we use the Food Demand program from section 1.9 above.

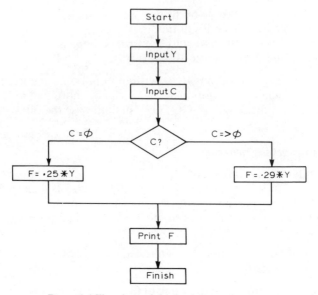

Figure 1.1 Flowchart of the food demand program

1.11 Loops (FOR . . . NEXT)

If we want to repeat part of a program, say a calculation, we call this a program *loop*. For instance, we might wish to calculate the average cost of different-sized loads of ready-mixed concrete. If we assume there is a delivery charge per load and then a charge per tonne for the actual concrete we can use the following program.

```
210 PRINT
220 PRINT "Delivery Charge (pounds) ";
230 INPUT D
240 PRINT
250 PRINT "Charge per Tonne (pounds) ";
260 INPUT P
270 PRINT

510 PRINT "Tonnes    Total Cost    Cost/Tonne"
520 PRINT
530 FOR T = 1 TO 10
540 C = D + P * T
550 A = C / T
560 PRINT T,C,A
570 NEXT T
580 PRINT
```

The two lines: 530 FOR T = 1 TO 10

and: 570 NEXT T

define a program loop.

When the program reaches line 530 it sets up a counter (T in this case) which is 1 for the first pass.

It then does whatever is on the lines between the FOR and the NEXT using the current value of T. So in this case it calculates the total cost (C) and the average cost (A) of 1 tonne of concrete.

The NEXT line adds 1 to T and sends it back to the FOR line. If T is <= 10 the calculation is carried out again.

So the loop continues for the values of T between 1 and 10, calculating and printing the number of tonnes, the total cost and the average cost each time.

Loops do not have to proceed in steps of 1 nor do they have to use ascending numbers. For instance we could get amounts from 10 tonnes to 1 tonne (instead of from 1 to 10) by substituting:

530 FOR T = 10 TO 1 STEP −1

The next section shows how loops are used with a new kind of variable to produce a common type of economic and business model.

1.12 Subscripted variables (arrays/vectors)

We very often want to hold a whole series of values of a variable for use in a program, such as income in different months. We usually use Y for income so we could call them Y1, Y2, Y3 and so on, with each year's income being a separate variable.

However, we often wish to refer to income in a general way, such as in a food demand model where food spending depended on the previous month's income.

Mathematically we show this as: $F_t = Y_{t-1} * 0.25$

we call t and $t-1$ *subscripts*, which in this model denote the present month (t), and the previous month ($t-1$).

So we can now amend the original food demand model to forecast food spending for the next six months if the user supplies six months income figures.

The lines to add to the program in section 1.4 are:

```
90   DIM Y(7)

225 FOR T = 1 TO 6
230 PRINT "Income in month ";T;"please ";
240 INPUT Y(T)
250 NEXT T

305 FOR T = 2 TO 7
310 F(T) = Y(T-1) * 0.25
320 NEXT T
```

```
520 PRINT "Month        Food Spending"
530 PRINT
540 FOR T = 2 TO 7
550 PRINT T,F(T)
560 NEXT T
570 PRINT
```

The 200 lines obtain the income for months 1–6.
The 300 lines calculate the food spending in each of months 2–7
   based on the previous month's income.
The 500 lines print out the food spending for months 2–7.

Two other points to note in this program are:

1. The use of the current value of T (the month) in the request for
INPUT in line 230).
2. Placing the heading for the results (line 520) outside the loop
prevents it being printed each time the loop is carried out.

   Variables which are *subscripted* are called *arrays* in computing,
and are often called *vectors* in economics. With loops they give
real power to computer models in economics, and we shall meet
them continually in the next eight chapters.

1.13 Data storage

All programs need data to work on. They get it in five ways:

1. Set up at the beginning of the program – such as M = 0.8. We
reserved lines 100–199 of our skeleton program for this.
2. Built into an expression in the program – such as F = Y ∗ 0.25 –
the 0.25 is necessary data for the line to work.
3. Supplied by the user – such as INPUT Y.
4. Obtained from a DATA FILE (on the computer but outside
the program we are currently using). We will not be using DATA
FILEs in this book mainly because they are handled differently on
different machines.
5. Contained within the program in a special section. This uses
another pair of special lines READ and DATA.

It is usual to put all the DATA lines together at the end of the
program, and we reserved lines 3000 onwards of our skeleton
program for them.
   As an example we might decide to put the figures for monthly
income for the section 1.12 version of the food demand program

within the program rather than input them. This could be done by changing the following lines:

230 (deleting this line as it is not needed)
240 READ Y(T)

3000 DATA 500,500,520
3010 DATA 520,540,530

Each time the program comes round to the READ line it looks for a value for Y(T) in the first available DATA line.

Each time it reads a data item it moves a pointer to the next item. So the DATA block is eventually used up. If there is not enough data, an error message will usually appear saying OUT OF DATA IN LINE 240. To use the data again you have to use the line RESTORE after the last READing of the data on most computers. How you put the DATA on the lines is not important to the computer, so write it in a form which makes checking easy.

1.14 Subroutines

If we need to use a few lines of program more than once in a program, it may be sensible to make them into a subroutine. They are put in a special section of the program (usually near the end) and written so that different parts of the program can use them. The best example in this book is the subroutine which will draw a graph of a variable. This SUBROUTINE is a large number of lines, often larger than the program itself, which can be added to almost any other program. On most computers, subroutines are used by a line saying GOSUB 2000 and at the end of the subroutine a line saying RETURN. On some computers such as the BBC micro, PROCEDURES are used which have some advantages over the GOSUB . . . RETURN method. If you wish to use subroutines, check with your computer manual how they are used on your machine.

1.15 Correcting programs

Very few people write a program which does not need 'improving'. Here are a few useful ideas:

1. Use some structure for all your programs. This could be as formal as the skeleton suggested in section 1.6, or a flowchart with line numbers written opposite the boxes, or just knowing where

you put certain operations. In each case, being methodical makes corrections easier.

2. Use regularly spaced line numbers. This leaves space for afterthoughts.

3. Most machines will renumber the lines if you run out of space, but remember that many of them renumber *all* the lines in the program, not just the ones you want changing.

4. Find out how to delete parts of lines while typing them. Usually there is a DELETE key, but on some machines you use a backwards arrow instead!

5. Whole lines can be deleted by retyping the line number.

6. A line is replaced by typing another line with the same number.

7. Most micros now have a facility for copying lines which are already on the screen. This can be useful if you only want to change one letter and you are not good at typing. It is also a useful way of changing line numbers without retyping the whole line.

1.16 Improving printed layouts

Screen or printed layouts can be improved by keeping them simple and uncluttered. Most of the programs in this book try to do this in three ways:

* Leaving blank lines between lines of output
* Spacing the output in columns using the TAB instruction. For instance:
    100 PRINT TAB(2);Q;TAB(12);Y
  will print the value of Q 2 spaces in from the left margin and the value of Y 12 spaces in.
* Rounding figures to 1 or 2 places of decimals. For instance:
    200 C = (INT(C*10+0.5))/10
  will round C to 1 place of decimals. It does this in three stages:
  1. multiplies C by 10 and adds 0.5
  2. takes the INTeger of this number (removes decimal places)
  3. divides by 10 (giving 1 decimal place)

1.17 Storing programs

To store a program on your computer it must of course have a cassette or disk! You type SAVE "abc" (abc being its name). Take care in saving programs because some computers do not check if you already have a program of this name stored. They just replace the original with the current one.

Further reading

There are an enormous number of quite good books on the market which will teach you BASIC. If you are only going to use one machine it is sensible in most cases to use the manual supplied with the machine.

EXERCISES

If you wish to practise BASIC as such, use some of the exercises from the BASIC manual you have chosen. If not, pass swiftly on to the next chapter where we introduce you (gently) to programming economic models.

Chapter 2

Basic economic relationships

2.1 Introduction

This chapter has two aims:

1. To develop your confidence in programming by building up some short BASIC programs in simple stages.
2. To explore a number of introductory economic concepts and relationships.

Our starting point is the important economic concept of opportunity cost, after which we move on to investigate a number of aspects of market demand. The computer programs demonstrate the use of PRINT and INPUT statements, and performing calculations in BASIC.

2.2 Opportunity cost

The starting point in economics is the recognition that we live in a world of scarcity. There are many competing demands on land, natural and human resources, and stocks of physical capital which we have at our disposal, and choices have to be made between them. Examining the nature of these choices is the very essence of our subject.

In many countries agricultural land is being lost as a result of encroachment from expanding towns and cities. Society has to choose the appropriate balance between town and countryside, as well as making choices about how it wants to use the agricultural land remaining. Land could be used for dairy cattle or for cereals, for instance, but certainly not for both at the same time. The conventional way to demonstrate such a choice is by means of a production possibility diagram (see Figure 2.1). We could produce 10 units of wheat if all the land were devoted to that particular use, or 20 units of milk if all the land were turned over to dairy herds. By devoting some land to each activity, we could produce any combination of milk and wheat along the production possibility

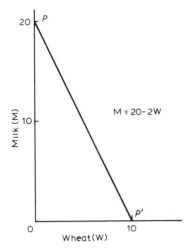

Figure 2.1 Production possibilities for milk and wheat

frontier *PP'*. For every additional unit of wheat grown two units of milk are lost, i.e. the opportunity cost of 1 wheat is 2 milk. In this example we have a linear frontier, so opportunity costs are constant.

Using the symbol W (for wheat) and M (for milk), the equation of *PP'* is:

$$M = 20 - 2W$$

This equation is incorporated into BASIC Program 2.1.

Program 2.1: Production possibilities with constant opportunity costs

```
>LIST

   100 PRINT
   110 PRINT "PRODUCTION POSSIBILITIES"
   120 PRINT "with CONSTANT COSTS"
   130 PRINT
   140 PRINT "Quantity of Wheat (1-9)    =";
   150 INPUT W
   160 M = 20 - 2*W
   170 PRINT "Quantity of Milk Possible = ";M
   995 END
>RUN

PRODUCTION POSSIBILITIES
with CONSTANT COSTS

Quantity of Wheat (1-9)    =?4
Quantity of Milk Possible = 12
```

Program notes

If you examine the program carefully you will see that it has a structure which is common to many programs.

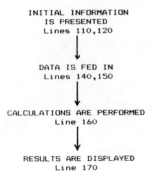

In Program 2.1 the first two lines print a heading. Line 140 prints a message asking us to decide the quantity of wheat to be produced. A semi-colon is placed at the end of this line to suppress the line feed, so the INPUT statement on line 150 puts a question mark on the *same* line as the printed text. Line 160 calculates the amount of milk that could be produced from the resources remaining. This line is the equation of the PP' frontier – note the use of the asterisk (*) to obtain the product. Line 170 prints out a message, and the value of M which was calculated in line 160. All printed text must be contained in quotes, but the quotes *must not* be used when the *value* of a variable, e.g. M, is being printed.

2.3 Increasing opportunity cost

The previous example assumes that land is homogeneous, so that the outputs from dairying and cereal growing are uniform irrespective of location. In reality, however, variations in climate and soil make some areas more suited to a particular product. The wetter areas are probably more suited to dairying, and drier areas to cereal production. In this case, the opportunity costs of wheat production will increase as it is extended. Less wheat will be grown and more milk lost as cereal production extends to the wetter areas. Figure 2.2 illustrates this increasing opportunity cost case.

The equation of the curve in Figure 2.2 is:

$$M = 20 \left(1 - \frac{W^2}{100}\right)^{0.5}$$

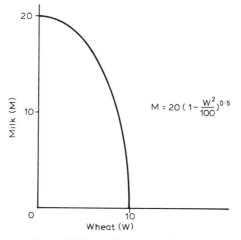

Figure 2.2 Increasing opportunity costs

This is incorporated in Program 2.2, where it appears in BASIC in the following form:

$$M1 = 20*(1-(W1 \uparrow 2/100)) \uparrow 0.5$$

You may like at this point to re-read section 1.5 (previous chapter), which explains BASIC arithmetic conventions.

Program 2.2: Production possibilities increasing costs

```
>LIST
 100 PRINT
 110 PRINT "PRODUCTION POSSIBILITIES"
 120 PRINT "with INCREASING COSTS"
 130 PRINT
 140 PRINT "Quantities of Wheat (1-9)"
 150 PRINT " 1st. Quantity = ";
 160 INPUT W1
 170 PRINT " 2nd. Quantity = ";
 180 INPUT W2
 190 M1 = 20*(1-(W1^2/100))^0.5
 200 M2 = 20*(1-(W2^2/100))^0.5
 219 REM**Calculates Opportunity Cost***********
 220 C = (M1-M2)/(W2-W1)
 300 PRINT
 310 PRINT "Quantities of Milk Possible"
 320 PRINT " 1st. Quantity = "; M1
 330 PRINT " 2nd. Quantity = "; M2
 340 PRINT
 350 PRINT "OPPORTUNITY COST:"
 360 PRINT " 1 Wheat costs ";C;" Milk"
 995 END
```

```
>RUN

PRODUCTION POSSIBILITIES
with INCREASING COSTS

Quantities of Wheat (1-9)
  1st. Quantity = ?4
  2nd. Quantity = ?5

Quantities of Milk Possible
  1st. Quantity = 18.3303028
  2nd. Quantity = 17.3205081

OPPORTUNITY COST:
  1 Wheat costs 1.0097947 Milk
```

Program notes

Program 2.2 enables us to input two levels of wheat output, and then calculates the amount of milk lost for every additional unit of wheat grown, i.e. the opportunity cost of wheat in terms of milk. By choosing pairs of values along the curve, we can confirm that increasing opportunity costs prevail.

If you feel that the string of decimals in the sample RUN for Program 1.2 makes it difficult to read, you could add the following lines. These will give the results to 2 decimal places.

```
238  REM **Converts results to ***********
239  REM **2 decimal places ***************
250  M1 = INT(100*M1 + 0.5)/100
260  M2 = INT(100*M2 + 0.5)/100
270  C = INT(100*C + 0.5)/100
```

For a particular set of production possibilities the combination of goods chosen will be influenced by the allocation system adopted. In our own economy the pattern of agricultural production is determined by a combination of market forces and official intervention. The factors determining free-market output levels and prices are explored in Chapter 3. The remainder of this chapter will prepare the ground for this, by exploring various aspects of market demand.

2.4 The economics of football – an example

In this section we shall develop a BASIC program to investigate a particular problem, and then show how the program can be modified to examine the general features of the demand for a product.

Investigation 1

A football club has a ground with a maximum capacity of 25 000 spectators. Following financial problems, the club recently raised its entrance fee from £2 to £3. As a result attendances have fallen to little over 17 000. The Board of Directors is split into two factions. One group wants to reduce the entrance fee to the previous level to bring the spectators back. The other group is in favour of still further increases.

A firm of market research consultants has estimated the following linear demand function for the club: Q = 25 000 − 2500*P.

Using this information, and a BASIC program, we have to discover what entrance fee the club should charge.

The BASIC program is developed in a series of distinct stages, starting with the relationship between price and quantity.

2.5 Price and quantity

The estimated demand curve for football attendance is shown in Figure 2.3.

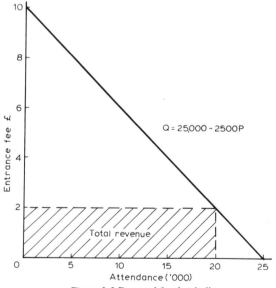

Figure 2.3 Demand for football

Attendance at different entrance fees can be calculated using Program 2.3.

Program 2.3: Football demand

```
LIST

     100 PRINT
     170 PRINT "FOOTBALL ATTENDANCE"
     180 PRINT
     260 PRINT "What is the Entrance Fee ";
     270 INPUT P
     310 Q = 25000-2500*P
     510 PRINT "Therefore the Estimated Attendance = ";Q
     995 END

>RUN

FOOTBALL ATTENDANCE

What is the Entrance Fee = ?2
Therefore the Estimated Attendance = 20000
```

Program notes

In the sample RUN for Program 2.3 a price of £2 has been entered. At this entrance fee the quantity (i.e. the level of football attendance) is 20000. By typing RUN, further prices can be tried.

2.6 Total revenue

In order to complete Investigation 1 we shall need to develop this program a stage further, so that it calculates income at different entrance fees. The football club's income, or total revenue (R), is the product of the entrance fee (P) and the attendance (Q). This can be expressed as:

$$R = P \times Q$$

This is calculated by the addition of the following lines to Program 2.3:

320 R = P*Q
530 PRINT "Football Club Income = ";R

It would also be sensible to add the Re-Run Option using the program lines 900 to 980 suggested in section 1.6 (Chapter 1). Various prices can then be tried until the revenue-maximizing one is found.

2.7 Generalizing the computer program

Program 2.3 is perfectly adequate to use for Investigation 1. What do we do, however, to answer other similar problems with *different* price and demand conditions? So long as the general procedure is the same, the program can be amended to allow for different values in the demand equation. In fact the main use of the computer is to perform repetitive operations using the same procedures with different data.

To generalize Program 2.3 it is necessary to replace the estimated demand equation for football with the following:

$$Q = A + B.P$$

A and B are called the *parameters* of the equation; in the football example they were 25 000 and −2500 respectively. Note that the values of price and quantity in the demand curve move in opposite directions (i.e. are inversely related), the value of B will be negative. Program 2.4 is the generalized version of Program 2.3 with the addition of the Total Revenue calculation.

Program 2.4: Linear demand

```
>LIST

100 PRINT
170 PRINT "LINEAR DEMAND STUDY."
175 PRINT
180 PRINT "Please specify your DEMAND EQUATION."
210 PRINT "Value of Intercept A (positive) = ";
220 INPUT A
230 PRINT "Value of Slope B (negative) = ";
240 INPUT B
250 PRINT
260 PRINT "What is your PRICE ";
270 INPUT P
280 PRINT
310 Q = A + B*P
320 R = P*Q
510 PRINT "Therefore the QUANTITY =";Q
520 PRINT "TOTAL REVENUE = ";P
995 END
```

Program notes

Program 2.4 differs from 2.3 in a number of respects. Lines 180 to 240 are concerned with the entry of values for the demand equation parameters, A and B. Line 310 incorporates the general form of the demand equation. The various PRINT statements have also been changed.

2.8 Price elasticity of demand

The price elasticity of demand is a measure of the responsiveness of demand to changes in price. For some products a small price change can induce relatively large changes in the quantity demanded. The demand for such products is said to be *elastic*. In other cases, where quite large price changes can leave demand relatively unaffected, demand is said to be *inelastic*.

Commodities with a large number of substitutes, such as particular brands of cheap confectionery, are likely to be price elastic, whereas those with few direct substitutes, such as electricity, tend to be price inelastic.

Price elasticity is given a numerical value using the following formula:

$$(-) \frac{\text{Proportional change in demand}}{\text{Proportional change in price}}$$

Using:

ΔQ to represent the change in demand;
Q for original demand;
ΔP for the change in price;
P for the original price;

the formula becomes:

$$\text{P.E.D.} = (-) \frac{\dfrac{\Delta Q}{Q}}{\dfrac{\Delta P}{P}} \text{ or } (-) \frac{\Delta Q}{\Delta P} \times \frac{P}{Q}$$

2.9 Point elasticity of demand

Price elasticity of demand can be measured for a particular point on the demand curve. If we imagine an infinitesimal movement along a demand curve then both ΔQ and ΔP will be very small, and $\Delta Q/\Delta P$ is the *slope* of the demand curve at a particular price and quantity combination. With the linear demand curve that we have been using the slope is the value of the parameter B, and the value of the point elasticity at any point on the demand curve is given by the simplified formula:

$$\text{P.E.D.} = -\,B \times \frac{P}{Q}$$

This calculation can be added to the linear demand Program 2.4 by incorporating the following lines:

```
330 E = -B*P/Q
530 PRINT "POINT ELASTICITY OF DEMAND = ";E
540 E = INT(100*E+0.5)/100
```

Program notes

With Program 2.4 so amended it is possible to:

1. Input the values for different linear demand functions;

2. Input a range of prices; although we must take care to ensure that the prices used are not so high that they generate *negative* quantities demanded. We can check the appropriate range by sketching a graph of each demand function before using it in the program.

3. Calculate and print out the quantity demanded, total revenue and point elasticity at various prices. Line 540 is optional. It gives the value of the elasticity to 2 decimal places.

A sample run of the amended Program 2.4 using data from Investigation 1 should appear as follows:

```
>RUN

LINEAR DEMAND STUDY

Please specify your DEMAND EQUATION.
Value of Intercept A (positive) = ?25000
Value of Slope B (negative) = ?-2500

What is your PRICE?2

Therefore the QUANTITY = 20000
TOTAL REVENUE = 40000
POINT ELASTICITY OF DEMAND = 0.25
```

As we are likely to want to use this program with different prices, while still retaining the same demand function, it is worthwhile adding the facility to loop back to Line 260 where the price is decided. This can be done by adding a conditional branching statement as follows:

```
610 PRINT "Do you want to choose another price (Y/N)";
620 INPUT Z$
630 IF Z$ = "Y" THEN GOTO 260
995 END
```

The variable Z$ will store any string of letters typed in from the keyboard. Line 630, however, tests to see whether the response is Y (short for Yes). If it is, the program will loop back to line 260 where another price can be selected. If any other letter is pressed the program will either end, or move on to the re-run option suggested in section 1.6 of the previous chapter, if you add the program lines 900–980 as suggested. In the latter case, you will be given the option of re-running the program from the beginning with new parameters in the demand function.

In the last four sections simple building blocks have been used to construct a useful program, which will enable us to investigate a number of important economic relationships. The full program is listed below.

Program 2.4a: Extended linear demand

```
$LIST

99  REM ** Extended version of Demand Program **********
100 PRINT
170 PRINT "LINEAR DEMAND STUDY."
175 PRINT
180 PRINT "Please specify your DEMAND EQUATION."
210 PRINT "Value of Intercept A (positive) = ";
220 INPUT A
230 PRINT "Value of Slope B (negative) = ";
240 INPUT B
250 PRINT
260 PRINT "What is your PRICE ";
270 INPUT P
310 Q = A + B*P
320 R = P*Q
330 E = B*P/Q
510 PRINT "Therefore the QUANTITY =";Q
520 PRINT "TOTAL REVENUE = ";R
530 PRINT "POINT ELASTICITY OF DEMAND =   ";E
540 E = INT(100*E+0.5)/100
610 PRINT "Do you want to choose another price (Y/N)";
620 INPUT Z$
630 IF Z$ = "Y" THEN 260
899 REM **Option to re-run program **********
900 PRINT
910 PRINT "Type 1 to END the program"
920 PRINT "     2 to RUN it again"
930 PRINT
940 INPUT Q9
950 IF Q9=1 THEN 990
960 IF Q9=2 THEN 100
970 PRINT "Please type 1 or 2"
980 GOTO 900
990 PRINT
995 PRINT "End of Program"
998 END
```

Program notes

Program 2.4a indicates how elements from the proposed program skeleton in section 1.6 can be incorporated in programs you write. It is assumed that the same re-run feature will be added to future programs, but for brevity the extra lines will be omitted from program listings.

2.10 Revenue and elasticity along the demand curve

Program 2.4a can now be used for our second investigation.

Investigation 2

This exercise starts with the simple demand function: $Q = 10 - P$ (i.e. $A = 10$ and $B = -1$). Prepare a table with the headings:

PRICE	QUANTITY	TOTAL REVENUE	POINT ELASTICITY
1			
2			
:			

Run Program 2.4a and record the values obtained for prices 1 up to 9 in the table. What do you observe about the changes in total revenue and point elasticity along the demand curve?

Re-run the program from the beginning, repeating the exercise with both an increased demand ($A = 20$), and a decreased demand ($A = 5$). Leave the slope of the demand function the same (i.e. $B = -1$) throughout. Do all three demand functions exhibit the same features? At what point on each demand curve is the total revenue maximized? Is the point elasticity constant at the same price on each demand curve? What price on a linear demand curve should a revenue maximizing firm seek?

When you have completed Investigation 2 you should have discovered the following interesting characteristics of the linear demand curve:

1. *Price elasticity varies along the demand curve*
Elasticity is unitary in the middle of the curve, becomes elastic at higher prices, and inelastic at lower prices. The value of the elasticity is infinity, i.e. perfectly elastic, at the point where the curve meets the price axis. Unfortunately the computer simply identifies a 'division by zero error' if a price of 10 is selected. This occurs because the denominator in the elasticity calculation is Q,

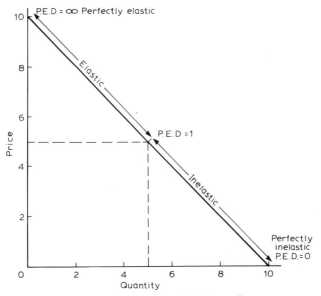

Figure 2.4 Price elasticity and the demand curve

which at this point on the demand curve is zero. At the lower end of the demand curve where the demand curve cuts the quantity axis, the price elasticity is zero – i.e. perfectly inelastic.

2. *Total revenue varies along the demand curve*
Total revenue is low both when prices are very high and when they are very low. In the former case, high prices mean low demand, and in the latter case high demand is achieved at very low prices. Total revenue reaches a peak when the quantity demanded corresponds with the mid-point of the demand curve, which incidentally occurs when the price elasticity is unity. Figure 2.5 illustrates the total revenue curve which corresponds with the demand function: $Q = 10 - P$. Sales on the horizontal axis correspond to the quantities demanded at prices between 0 and 10.

Figure 2.5 Total revenue and sales

EXERCISES

(**2.1**) Use Program 2.2 to investigate the principle of increasing opportunity costs. Prepare a table and record the opportunity cost of each unit of wheat from the 2nd to the 9th. Input quantities 1 and 2 for the cost of the second unit, 2 and 3 for the cost of the third, and so on. Change the values 20 and 100 in the equation, and see what happens to the relationship.

(2.2) Graph the results obtained from the Football Program 2.3 and show total revenue at different levels of attendance. At what price is total revenue at a maximum?

Why does it not necessarily pay a football club to aim for maximum attendances?

(2.3) Use Program 2.4a to investigate the relationship between total revenue and point elasticity along the following demand curves:

$$QD = 100 - 2P$$
$$QD = 50 - 2P$$
$$QD = 50 - 0.5P$$
$$QD = 75 - P$$

Sketch each curve on graph paper before you carry out the exercise. What pattern emerges?

(2.4) Arc elasticity measures the elasticity of demand for discrete movements along the demand curve, e.g. when a price rise from 8 to 12 results in a fall in demand from 120 to 90. Two formulae are commonly employed for arc elasticity.

A base point formula:

$$P.E.D. = - \frac{\left(\dfrac{\text{Change in demand}}{\text{Original demand}} \right)}{\left(\dfrac{\text{Change in price}}{\text{Original price}} \right)} = - \frac{\left(\dfrac{90 - 120}{90} \right)}{\left(\dfrac{12 - 8}{12} \right)}$$

A mid-point formula:

$$P.E.D. = - \frac{\left(\dfrac{\text{Change in demand}}{\text{Average demand}} \right)}{\left(\dfrac{\text{Change in price}}{\text{Average price}} \right)} = - \frac{\left(\dfrac{90 - 120}{105} \right)}{\left(\dfrac{12 - 8}{10} \right)}$$

Write a program which enables you to input 2 values for price and quantity and calculates the arc elasticity using both methods. Compare the results obtained from each formula for price increases and decreases over the same range.

Chapter 3

The market mechanism

3.1 Introduction

This chapter explores demand and supply analysis; the economist's tool for understanding the operation of markets. The computer programs developed within the chapter include illustrations of the following operations in BASIC:

READ . . . DATA statements
FOR . . . NEXT loops
Arrays and DIM statements
Print formatting using TAB
Subroutines

3.2 The market mechanism

Markets provide a system of decentralized decision making, in which commodities are allocated by a series of exchange transactions between consumers and producers. Each group is assumed to be guided by self-interest. Individual consumers set out to maximize utility, the economists' term for satisfaction or well-being, and producers seek to maximize profits. All goods have *prices*, which are determined by the interaction of the forces of demand and supply. It is generally assumed that free market prices will adjust to the minimum level which enables the market to *clear*. Market clearing occurs when the quantity that firms are willing and able to supply exactly matches the quantities that consumers are willing and able to buy at the ruling price. The study of how prices are determined in such markets is a significant component of *micro-economics*, the branch of economics which examines decision-making at the level of economic units and markets.

3.3 Demand, supply and equilibrium price

Demand for a product is determined by its price. In general the higher the price, the lower will be the level of demand. As we established in the previous chapter, the sign on this relationship is negative, and the demand curve slopes down from left to right. When expressing the basic price-quantity relationship of the demand function we shall use the general form: $QD = A + B.P.$ (where $B<0$).

Demand is affected by a number of factors other than price, such as income levels, the prices of related products, and consumer tastes and preferences. As these change then so do the underlying conditions of demand, and the price-quantity relationship underlying the demand curve will *shift*. Using the variable $S1$ to represent demand shifts, our demand equation becomes: $QD = A + S1 + B.P.$ So long as the conditions of demand remain unchanged, the value of $S1$ will be zero.

Supply is also affected by price. Higher prices will cover higher costs of production; existing producers will be able to expand and new producers enter the market. The sign on the relationship between price and supply is positive, and the supply curve slopes upwards from left to right (see Figure 3.1).

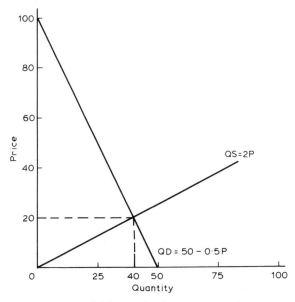

Figure 3.1 Demand and supply equilibrium

The supply function can also be shifted by changes in factors other than price. Changes in production costs, the state of technology, the levels of taxes and subsidies, and the relative prices and profitability of alternative products will all cause supply to shift. The variable *S2* will be used to represent supply shifts, so the general form of our supply equation becomes: $QS = C + S2 + D.P$. The intercept is $(C + S2)$, with *S2* normally taking on the value of zero, and the slope is *D* (where *D>0*).

Equilibrium price is the level of price which equates demand and supply. Figure 3.1 illustrates demand and supply curves derived from the following equations:

$$QD = 50 - 0.5P \quad (A=50,\ S1=0,\ B=-0.5)$$
$$QS = 2P \quad\quad\quad (C=0,\ S2=0,\ D=2)$$

The condition for equilibrium is that $QD = QS$, and this occurs at a price of 20 and a quantity of 40. At prices below 20 there would be an *excess demand* and the price would rise; whereas prices above 20 would lead to an *excess supply* and the price would fall.

In writing a program to determine the equilibrium price and quantity in different demand and supply conditions, the first stage is to input values for the demand and supply functions. This involves extending the procedure used in Program 2.4a to include the parameters of the supply function. For the remainder of the program, two alternative approaches could be used.

1. *An iterative approach*

This involves working in a step-by-step way towards a solution. A price is selected, and the program calculates the levels of both demand and supply at this price. A test for the equality of demand and supply is then applied. If they are different, there is the opportunity to try other prices; otherwise the computer prints out a message to say that the equilibrium has been found. This approach is demonstrated in Program 3.1a.

Program 3.1a: Demand and supply – iterative approach

```
>LIST

100 PRINT
110 S1=0:S2=0
170 PRINT TAB(4);"DEMAND & SUPPLY EQUILIBRIUM"
175 PRINT
180 PRINT "Please specify your DEMAND EQUATION."
210 PRINT "Value of Intercept A (positive) = ";
220 INPUT A
230 PRINT "Value of Slope B (negative) = ";
240 INPUT B
245 PRINT
250 PRINT "Please specify your SUPPLY EQUATION."
255 PRINT "Value of Intercept C = ";
260 INPUT C
265 PRINT "Value of Slope D (positive) = ";
270 INPUT D
275 PRINT
```

```
310 PRINT "PRICE";TAB(15)"QD";TAB(30);"QS"
320 INPUT P
325 REM**CALCULATES D & S *****
330 QD = A+S1+B*P
340 QS = C+S2+D*P
350 REM**CONVERTS TO 1 DECIMAL PLACE**
360 QD = INT(10*QD+0.5)/100
370 QS = INT(10*QS+0.5)/100
510 PRINT TAB(14);QD;TAB(29);QS
520 IF QD<>QS THEN GOTO 320
525 PRINT
530 PRINT TAB(4);"THIS IS THE EQUILIBRIUM !"
995 END
```

The sample run following uses the values for the demand and supply functions from section 3.3.

```
>RUN

        DEMAND & SUPPLY EQUILIBRIUM

Please specify your DEMAND EQUATION.
Value of Intercept A (positive) = ?50
Value of Slope B (negative) = ?-0.5

Please specify your SUPPLY EQUATION.
Value of Intercept C = ?0
Value of Slope D (positive) = ?2

PRICE           QD              QS
?10
                45              20
?20
                40              40

    THIS IS THE EQUILIBRIUM !
```

Program notes

Line 110 sets the values of the shift variables to zero. Lines 180 to 270 are concerned with inputting the parameters of the demand and supply equations. In lines 310 and 510 the TAB function is used to position the results under appropriate headings. Note how the values are rounded to one decimal place in lines 360 and 370 *before* the test for equilibrium is applied in line 520. If the answers came to numerous decimal places and we relied on a test of equality to determine equilibrium, then it would probably be necessary to input many prices before we discovered the one which was exactly correct to the appropriate number of decimal places. Rounding to one decimal place before applying the test makes it easier to find the answer. You will see that line 520 loops the program back to line 320, if we have not found the equilibrium. This gives us another attempt to find the correct price.

2. An analytical approach

The iterative approach, while interesting, is not appropriate if we want to establish the equilibrium immediately. In this case, we need to incorporate an analytical solution to the problem into our program. Such a solution is derived in the following way:

Demand: $\qquad QD = A+S1+B.P$
Supply: $\qquad QS = C+S2+D.P$
But in equilibrium: $\qquad QD = QS$
So,

$$A+S1+B.P = C+S2+D.P$$
$$B.P-D.P = C-A+S2-S1$$
$$P(B-D) = C-A+S2-S1$$

Therefore the *equilibrium price* is:

$$P = \frac{C-A+S2-S1}{B-D}$$

Substituting into the demand equation gives the *equilibrium quantity*. Which can either be expressed in terms of P:

$$Q = C+S2+D.P$$

Or in terms of the parameters:

$$Q = C+S2+D \left(\frac{C-A+S2-S1}{B-D} \right)$$

These general solutions can be incorporated into a program in the following way.

Program 3.1b: Demand and supply – analytical solution

Begin by deleting lines 310 to 530 from Program 3.1a, then add the following lines:

```
100 REM** D&S ANALYTICAL APPROACH ***
310 P = (C−A+S2−S1)/(B−D)
320 Q = C+S2+D*P
510 PRINT "Equilibrium Price    = ";P
520 PRINT "Equilibrium Quantity = ";Q
```

Now that we have worked out this general analytical solution for equilibrium, we shall be able to use it in a number of programs.

3.4 Do we need theories of demand and supply?

Demand and supply analysis is concerned with the study of price formation in free markets. In common with most studies within economics, we tend to justify our activities in one of two ways:

1. The desire to explain the behaviour observed within markets for its own sake. This is a normal manifestation of the process of intellectual curiosity.

2. The need to derive predictions about likely future movements in the size of a particular market and prevailing price levels. These would form a basis for advice to firms, financial institutions and governments on purely practical matters.

With regard to the latter, students must wonder at times why theoretical models must be constructed to answer the pragmatic concerns of everyday economic life. Surely perfectly adequate predictions can be derived using quite elementary statistical techniques. The relationship between market price and sales is apparently a good illustration of this. When called upon to advise on pricing policy an economist would have access to past data on prices and sales, so, after making some adjustment to prices to allow for the effects of inflation, it is a relatively simple matter to derive a relationship which could provide a basis for forecasting. Past sales data would enable us to fit a line corresponding to the demand curve (see Figure 3.2); this line could then be used for market predictions. The techniques for doing this are developed in Chapter 4.

Time period	Price	Quantity
1	30	5
2	25	12·5
3	20	20
4	15	27·5
5	10	35

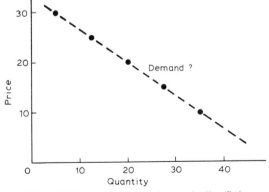

Figure 3.2 Deriving a demand curve by line fitting

Unfortunately, things are not quite as easy as this. Although a series of price/sales figures might possibly yield the demand curve for the product, more often than not they will bear little relationship to the true demand curve. The data could, for instance, have been generated by a series of shifts in both the demand and supply conditions (see Figure 3.3), in which case we would be no nearer to knowing the position of the true demand curve. There is what econometricians call an *identification problem*. The only way we can begin to come to terms with this is to have a full demand and supply model which takes account of all the major factors influencing the market. The specific relationship between, say, price and quantity can then be solved simultaneously.

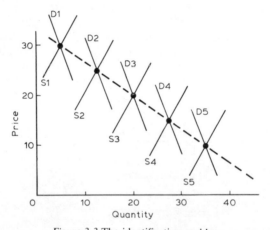

Figure 3.3 The identification problem

Once allowance is made for both demand and supply conditions changing, it is clear that price and sales data can take on any form. They could even produce an apparently upward sloping demand curve.

Program 3.2 generates the series of equilibrium price-quantity combinations shown in Figures 3.2 and 3.3, in response to pre-programmed shifts in the demand and supply equations. The program employs the analytical solution from Program 3.1b, with the following specific demand and supply equations:

$$QD = 20-0.5P+S1 \quad (A=20, B=-0.5)$$
$$QS = -10+0.5P+S2 \quad (C=-10, D=0.5)$$

Program 3.2: The identification problem

```
>LIST

49  REM ***Price and Quantity Arrays **************
50  DIM P(5),Q(5)
100 PRINT
109 REM *** Demand & Supply Parameters ********
110 A=20:B=-0.5:C=-10:D=0.5
180 PRINT TAB(4);"THE IDENTIFICATION PROBLEM"
190 PRINT
300 FOR T = 1 TO 5
309 REM ***Read Demand & Supply Shift ************
310 READ S1,S2
320 P(T) = (C-A+S2-S1)/(B-D)
330 Q(T) =   C+S2+D*P(T)
340 NEXT T
500 PRINT "Time";TAB(14);"Price";TAB(28);"Quantity"
510 PRINT
520 FOR T = 1 TO 5
530 PRINT TAB(2);T;TAB(15);P(T);TAB(30);Q(T)
540 NEXT T
995 END
2999 REM *** Value of Demand & Supply Shifts *******
3000 DATA 0,0
3010 DATA 5,10
3020 DATA 10,20
3030 DATA 15,30
3040 DATA 20,40

>RUN
```

```
    THE IDENTIFICATION PROBLEM

Time          Price        Quantity

1             30           5
2             25           12.5
3             20           20
4             15           27.5
5             10           35
```

Program notes

The FOR . . . NEXT loop between lines 300 and 340 reads, in turn, 5 pairs of values for *S1* and *S2*, the shift parameters in the demand and supply equations, and computes values for price and quantity.

These values are stored in two arrays: one with 5 values for price, and the other with 5 values for quantity. Line 50 informs the computer of the dimension of these arrays, so that space can be reserved in the computer's memory for storage. The program loop between lines 520 and 540 is concerned with printing out the price-quantity combinations for each time period.

3.5 The incidence of a sales tax

Governments levy taxes on commodities in order to either raise revenue or discourage consumption. If revenue raising is the principal motive it is necessary to find goods for which demand is relatively inelastic; whereas if the goal is to discourage consumption it is desirable to have a relatively elastic demand. In each case the government would want to know the effect of the tax on both the price of the commodity and the quantity sold.

When a tax is levied on a commodity it has to be paid for by either consumers, or producers, or both. The division of the payment between these two groups is known as the *incidence* of the tax. It is easily demonstrated that the incidence of a tax depends upon the slopes of the demand and supply curves. For simplicity we shall use the example of a specific excise duty of so many pence – the type of duty which tends to be levied on alcoholic drinks. Such a duty raises the costs of supply by the amount of the tax. In Figure 3.4 this is represented by a vertical shift in the supply curve from *S1* to *S2*. The incidence of the tax on consumers (*IC*) is *P2−P1*, the extent of the price rise; the incidence on producers (*IP*) is the remainder *T−IC*.

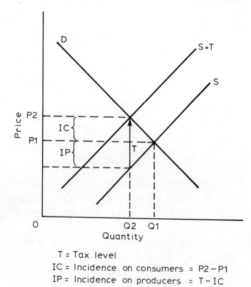

T = Tax level
IC = Incidence on consumers = P2 − P1
IP = Incidence on producers = T − IC

Figure 3.4 The incidence of a specific excise tax

Program 3.3 is designed to investigate the effects of changes in the slopes of the demand and supply curves upon the relative incidence. The program employs the same basic demand and supply model that we have used throughout this chapter. Before proceeding, however, it is necessary to draw attention to the way in which the tax shifts the supply curve. Although the supply curve is shifted vertically up the *price* axis by the tax, the intercept on the supply curve relates to the quantity axis. Given that the supply curve has a slope of D, a shift up the price axis of T becomes a negative shift along the quantity axis of $T \times D$. So, the shift variable in the supply equation becomes:

$$S2 = -T \times D$$

Program 3.3: The incidence of a specific tax

```
>LIST

50   DIM P(2),Q(2)
100  PRINT
109  REM **Fix the demand & supply intercepts *****
110  S1=0:S2=0:A=100:C=0
170  PRINT TAB(5); "THE INCIDENCE OF A TAX."
175  PRINT
210  PRINT "DEMAND CURVE:"
220  PRINT " Value of Slope B (negative) = ";
230  INPUT B
240  PRINT "SUPPLY CURVE:"
250  PRINT " Value of Slope D (positive) = ";
260  INPUT D
265  PRINT
270  N=1
280  GOSUB 1000: REM **Calculate Equilibrium *******
290  PRINT "BEFORE TAX:"
300  PRINT " Equilibrium Price = ";P(1)
310  PRINT " Equilibrium Quantity = ";Q(1)
315  PRINT
320  PRINT "Level of SPECIFIC TAX = ";
330  INPUT T
340  S2 =-T*D
350  N=2
360  GOSUB 1000: REM **Calculate Equilibrium *******
370  REM** Calculate incidence ***********
380  IC=P(2)-P(1)
390  IP=T-IC
400  IC=INT(IC*100+0.5)/100
410  IP=INT(IP*100+0.5)/100
510  PRINT
520  PRINT "AFTER TAX:"
530  PRINT " New Equilibrium Price = ";P(2)
540  PRINT " New Equilibrium Quantity = ";Q(2)
545  PRINT
550  PRINT "TAX INCIDENCE:"
560  PRINT " On Consumers = ";IC
570  PRINT " On Producers = ";IP
990  END
998  REM**Sub-routine to calculate*********
999  REM*Equilib to 2 decimal places*********
1000 P(N)=(C-A+S2-S1)/(B-D)
1010 Q(N)=C+S2+D*P(N)
1020 P(N)=INT(P(N)*100+0.5)/100
1030 Q(N)=INT(Q(N)*100+0.5)/100
1040 RETURN

>RUN

     THE INCIDENCE OF A TAX

DEMAND CURVE:
 Value of Slope B (negative) = ?-1
SUPPLY CURVE:
 Value of Slope D (positive) = ?1
```

```
BEFORE TAX:
  Equilibrium Price    = 50
  Equilibrium Quantity = 50

Level of SPECIFIC TAX = ?10

AFTER TAX:
  New Equilibrium Price    = 55
  New Equilibrium Quantity = 45

TAX INCIDENCE:
  On Consumers = 5
  On Producers = 5
```

Program notes

In line 110 the initial values of the shift variables are set to zero, the quantity intercept on the demand curve is set to 100, and on the supply curve to zero. To change these each time we run the program would be a distraction, especially when we want to concentrate on the effects of changes in slope on the incidence. Values for price and quantity before and after the tax are stored in two arrays, which are dimensioned in line 50. The program uses a subroutine at line 1000 to calculate price and quantity to two decimal places. Setting N=1 in line 270 and N=2 in line 350, before each call to the subroutine numbers the elements of each array to represent the values before and after the tax. Line 340 converts the tax into a quantity supply shift.

Line 380 defines the incidence of the tax on consumers as the rise in price, and 390 calculates the incidence on producers as the difference between the tax and the consumer incidence.

3.6 The dynamic theory of price

The demand and supply examples presented in the first part of this chapter were based upon what economists call *comparative static analysis*. We established the prevailing price and quantity for a given set of demand and supply conditions, and then calculated the new equilibrium which resulted from a change in the underlying conditions. In our models the changes were represented by the shift parameters *S1* and *S2*, and it was implicitly assumed throughout that the market would adjust instantaneously to the new conditions.

In many markets, however, there are significant 'time lags' between decisions to produce and the final product being available. This is especially true of agricultural markets, where production lags can be very long indeed: 6 to 9 months for temperate food crops, 2 years or more for livestock, and as long as 5 to 7 years for tropical tree crops such as coffee and rubber. In such cases the demand and supply model must allow for a *lagged adjustment* in the supply equation. Current supply will tend to reflect the price conditions ruling in the market at the time the production decision was made. The modified demand and supply model will appear as follows:

Demand: $D_t = A + S1 + B.P_t$
Supply: $S_t = C + S2 + D.P_{t-1}$
For Equilibrium: $D_t = S_t$

where the subscript t represents the current time period, and $t-1$ represents the previous time period.

With a lagged model of this type, it could be some time before the market settles down to a new equilibrium once it has been disturbed. Conditions such as these are portrayed in the familiar *cobweb diagram* (see Figure 3.5). If the market equilibrium is

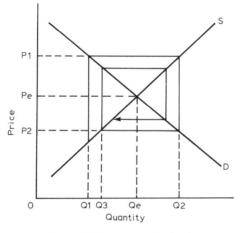

Figure 3.5 A convergent cobweb

disturbed by a one period fall in supply to Q1 which leads to price rising to P1, the following chain reaction will follow. Suppliers will plan to produce quantity Q2 in the next period, whereupon price will fall to P2. This will cause planned supply to fall further to Q3, and the process will continue *ad infinitum* unless corrected. The obvious corrective mechanism in such a situation is learning. Once producers realize what is happening they will presumably take account of such cycles in making production decisions. The evidence from agricultural markets, however, does suggest that instability can persist for a considerable time.

Depending upon the relative slopes of the demand and supply curves, cobweb cycles can take on three forms:

1. *Convergent* – when there is a progressive movement towards the equilibrium.
2. *Divergent* – when the movement is away from the equilibrium.
3. *Stable* – a uniform cycle which is neither diverging nor converging.

Program 3.4 is designed to explore the circumstances which produce each of these types of cycle.

Program 3.4: The cobweb cycle

```
>LIST

50   DIM P(10),Q(10)
100  PRINT
110  A=100 : C=0 : S1=0 : S2=0
120  REM** Define function for 1 place of decimals **********
130  DEF FND(V)=INT(10*V+0.5)/10
170  PRINT TAB(10);"THE COBWEB THEOREM."
180  PRINT
200  PRINT "DEMAND CURVE:"
210  PRINT " Value of Slope B (negative) = ";
220  INPUT B
230  PRINT "SUPPLY CURVE:"
240  PRINT " Value of Slope D (positive) = ";
250  INPUT D
260  PRINT
270  REM ** Calculate Equilibrium ************
280  P(0)=(C-A+S2-S1)/(B-D)
290  Q(0)=C+S2+D*P(0)
300  PRINT "Equilibrium Price    = ";FND(P(0))
310  PRINT "Equilibrium Quantity = ";FND(Q(0))
315  PRINT
320  PRINT "Now introduce a shock into the system."
325  PRINT
330  PRINT "  NEW QUANTITY = ";
340  INPUT Q(1)
350  PRINT
359  REM ** Calculate Cobweb Series ************
360  FOR T = 1 TO 9
370  P(T) = (Q(T)-A-S1)/B
380  Q(T+1)= C+S2+D*P(T)
390  NEXT T
500   PRINT "Period";TAB(10);"Price";TAB(20);"Quantity"
510  FOR T=0 TO 9
520  PRINT TAB(3);T;TAB(10);FND(P(T));TAB(22);FND(Q(T))
530  NEXT T
540  PRINT
995  END


>RUN

        THE COBWEB THEOREM.

DEMAND CURVE:
 Value of Slope B (negative) = ?-1
SUPPLY CURVE:
 Value of Slope D (positive) = ?1
```

```
Equilibrium Price    = 50
Equilibrium Quantity = 50

Now introduce a shock into the system.

 NEW QUANTITY = 60

Period    Price      Quantity
   0       50          50
   1       40          60
   2       60          40
   3       40          60
   4       60          40
   5       40          60
   6       60          40
   7       40          60
   8       60          40
```

Program notes

Program 3.4 has the following stages:

1. The intercepts on the demand and supply curves are fixed at 100 and 0 respectively in line 110.
2. The slopes of the curves are selected in lines 200 to 250, which are borrowed from Program 3.3.
3. Lines 280 to 310 calculate and print out the equilibrium price and quantity.
4. A shock is introduced into the system, e.g. the effects of a poor harvest, by INPUTing a quantity which is different from the equilibrium one (lines 320–340).
5. Price and quantity are calculated for the subsequent 9 time periods. P_t is used to calculate the quantity, Q_{t+1} in the FOR . . . NEXT loop between lines 360 and 390.
6. The results are displayed in tabular form (Lines 500–530).
7. By adding a re-run option the process can be repeated using demand and supply curves with different slopes.

In line 130 a function has been defined to round variables to one place of decimals. This procedure saves us having to repeat the same coding for each variable to be printed out. Instead we can perform FND (the decimal places function) on any variable, see lines 300, 310 and 520.

Use of the graphics subroutine

This cobweb program can be used with the graphics subroutine listed in the Appendix. The routines are machine specific, so it will be necessary to load in the routine which is designed for your computer *before* you type in Program 3.4. The routine will produce a graph of the movements in price over the 10 time periods, making it immediately obvious whether the cobweb is convergent, divergent or stable. The following lines must be added to your program to enable your data to be transferred to the subroutine.

```
60   DIM Y(10)
130  Y$="PRICE"
140  MT=10
375  Y(T) = P(T)
550  PRINT "PRESS <RETURN> FOR A GRAPH";
560  INPUT R$
570  GOSUB 2000
```

3.7 Producer cooperatives and government marketing boards

In the farming sector, which is particularly vulnerable to price fluctuations, a number of stabilization schemes have been devised. In some countries farmers have banded together to form *producer cooperatives*, in an attempt to gain more influence upon the market for their produce. Such cooperatives have been particularly important in Denmark, for instance, where dairy and pig farmers organize the marketing of their produce on a collective basis. By coordinating their actions in this way farmers are able to influence the market price they receive for their produce. In order to prevent prices from falling when supplies are large, the cooperative can stockpile any excess supply. When production is down, the stockpiles can be released, to prevent excessive price increases. By operating such a system of *buffer stocks*, the cooperative can help to stabilize both the prices paid by customers and the incomes received by farmers.

Cooperative buffer stocks is a voluntary scheme operated by farmers themselves. Other stabilization schemes entail direct government involvement. Systems of guaranteed prices and direct income support operate in many countries. Government-controlled *marketing boards* purchase produce from farmers at guaranteed price levels, and themselves operate buffer stock schemes similar to those of the cooperative. There is, however, a significant difference between the two types of scheme. Under cooperative arrangements, farmers are usually paid for their produce when it is finally sold. In a year when output is high, a controlled amount is sold and any surplus stockpiled. Incomes accrue to farmers only from part of the production which is sold. With a government marketing board controlled scheme, however, the entire supply would be brought up at the guaranteed price. Consequently under a cooperative scheme both prices and incomes are stabilized, whereas under the marketing board scheme, although price is stabilized, incomes tend to vary directly with the size of the harvest (see Figure 3.6). Price stabilization under a producers' cooperative is simulated in Program 3.5.

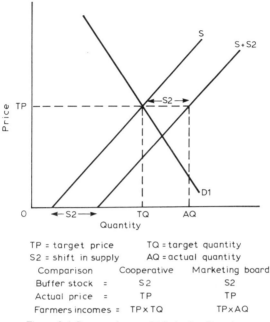

Comparison	Cooperative	Marketing board
Buffer stock =	S2	S2
Actual price =	TP	TP
Farmers incomes =	TP×TQ	TP×AQ

Figure 3.6 Cooperatives and Marketing Boards

Program 3.5: Buffer stocks and the producers cooperative

```
>LIST
     49   REM**Output,Price,Expected & Actual Income*****
     50   DIM Q(12),P(12),EI(12),AI(12)
     59   REM**Stocks,Expected Price,Market Supply*********
     60   DIM S(12),EP(12),MS(12)
    100   PRINT
    119   REM**Demand and Supply Parameters*****
    120   A=250 : B=-1 : S1=0
    130   C=125 : D=0.5 : S2=0
    140   S(5)=0
    149   REM** Rounds to nearest integer *************
    150   DEF FND(V)=INT(V+0.5)
    170   PRINT TAB(5); "COOPERATIVE BUFFER STOCKS"
    180   PRINT
    190   PRINT "The Demand for Butter is represented by"
    200   PRINT "the equation: QD= 250 - P"
    210   PRINT "In the past 5 years the market"
    220   PRINT "has fluctuated as follows:"
    230   PRINT
    239   REM** Prints table of last 5 years **************
    240   PRINT "YEAR";TAB(7);"OUTPUT";TAB(17);"PRICE";TAB(25);"FARM
```

```
INCOMES"
  250 FOR T=1 TO 5
  260 S2=100*RND(1)
  270 P(T)=(C-A+S2-S1)/(B-D)
  280 Q(T)=C+S2+D*P(T)
  290 AI(T)=FND(P(T))*FND(Q(T))
  300 PRINT TAB(2);T;TAB(8);FND(Q(T));TAB(18);FND(P(T));
TAB(28);FND(AI(T))
  310 NEXT T
  320 PRINT
  330 PRINT "A farmers' cooperative is formed"
  340 PRINT "to stabilise the market using"
  350 PRINT "buffer stocks. As the manager,"
  360 PRINT "you will have information about"
  370 PRINT "current production and stock levels."
  380 PRINT "   Target Price  = 50"
  390 PRINT "   TARGET INCOME = 10000"
  400 PRINT
  410 PRINT TAB(5); "PRESS <RETURN> TO CONTINUE";
  420 INPUT R$
  429 REM** Begins decisions loop *********
  430 FOR T=6 TO 12
  440 PRINT
  450 PRINT "YEAR ";T
  460 PRINT
  469 REM** Calculates expected position*********
  470 S2=100*RND(1)
  480 EP(T)=(C-A+S2-S1)/(B-D)
  490 Q(T)=C+S2+D*EP(T)
  500 EI(T)=FND(Q(T))*FND(EP(T))
  510 PRINT "Target Supply      = 200"
  520 PRINT "Current Production = ";FND(Q(T))
  530 PRINT "Expected Price     = ";FND(EP(T))
  540 PRINT "EXPECTED INCOME    = ";EI(T)
  550 PRINT "Stocks             = ";S(T-1)
  560 PRINT
  570 PRINT "Planned Change in Stocks:"
  580 PRINT "use (-)minus for decrease";
  590 INPUT DS
  600 IF S(T-1)+DS>=0 THEN GOTO 640
  610 PRINT "You do not have this level
  620 PRINT "of stock to release."
  630 GOTO 560
  640 PRINT
  649 REM**Calculates results of action**********
  650 S(T)=S(T-1)+DS
  660 MS(T)=FND(Q(T))-DS
  670 P(T)=(MS(T)-A-S1)/B
  680 AI(T)=FND(MS(T))*FND(P(T))
  690 PRINT "New stock level = ";S(T)
  700 PRINT "Actual Supply   = ";FND(MS(T))
  710 PRINT "Actual Price    = ";FND(P(T))
  720 PRINT "ACTUAL INCOME   = ";AI(T)
  730 NEXT T
  995 END

>RUN

     COOPERATIVE BUFFER STOCKS

The Demand for Butter is represented by
the equation: QD= 250 - P
In the past 5 years the market
has fluctuated as follows:

YEAR   OUTPUT   PRICE     FARM INCOMES
  1      168      82         13776
  2      221      29          6409
  3      216      34          7344
  4      188      62         11656
  5      213      37          7881
```

```
A farmers' cooperative is formed
to stabilise the market using
buffer stocks. As the manager,
you will have information about
current production and stock levels.
   Target Price  = 50
   Target Income = 10000

     PRESS <RETURN> TO CONTINUE?

YEAR 6

Target Supply        = 200
Current Production = 204
Expected Price       = 46
EXPECTED INCOME      = 9384
Stocks               = 0

Planned Change in Stocks:
use (-)minus for decrease?4

New stock level = 4
Actual Supply   = 200
Actual Price    = 50
ACTUAL INCOME   = 10000
```

Program notes

A number of features of the model are worthy of note. Market supply is determined by production and the change in stock levels (line 660). The values are chosen such that supply fluctuates around the market equilibrium of 200, which yields a price of 50 and normal income level of 10000. You can check this by calculating the equilibrium price and quantity from the parameters of the demand and supply equations which are given in lines 120 and 130.

Use is made throughout the program of the function defined in line 140, which rounds to the nearest whole number.

The program reinforces a few simple lessons:

1. A cooperative can have no influence whatsoever on the market until it has accumulated some buffer stocks with which to operate.
2. Stocks should be increased when production is above target levels, and released to make up for shortfalls in supply.
3. Both prices and incomes should be more stable with a cooperative buffer stocks policy than without one.

EXERCISES

(3.1) (a) What factors could cause the demand curve for a product to shift?
(b) What factors could cause supply to shift?
(c) Change the data statements in Program 3.2 to do the following:

(i) shift demand over 5 periods, leaving supply unchanged.
(ii) shift supply over 5 periods, leaving demand unchanged.
Which curve is identified from the equilibrium prices and quantities in each case?
(iii) Try a combination of different demand and supply shifts and plot the resulting equilibria on a scatter graph.

(3.2) Use Program 3.3 to establish the circumstances in which the incidence of a specific sales tax will fall most heavily upon consumers.

(3.3) Run the Cobweb Program 3.4 with the following values for the slopes B and D:

B	D
-1.5	1
-1	1.5
-5	2
-2	5
-1	1

Each time you run the program graph the demand and supply curves, and mark out the resulting cobweb. Under what circumstances does the cobweb:
(a) converge,
(b) diverge,
(c) produce a regular oscillation?

(3.4) Producers' cooperatives can work to *stabilize* farmers incomes, but if they try to *raise* incomes by restricting supply they break down. Use Program 3.5 to investigate the effects of maintaining prices above the level of 50 – the market equilibrium. What happens to buffer stock levels? (Hint: it will help if you calculate a new target supply, by reading a higher price into the demand equation.)

(3.5) Modify Program 3.5 so that it simulates the operations of a government marketing board.

Chapter 4

Demand forecasting

4.1 Two approaches to forecasting

In general, methods of forecasting can all be divided into two groups, those which use a *model* and those which do not. If they use a model they have an explanation of *why* demand will change. As we saw in Chapter 3, people may buy more because their incomes go up, or they may buy less because prices go up. In both cases we have a 'scientific' explanation which seems reasonable in the light of what we know about people.

If we do not have a model of how customers behave we may still be able to forecast the sales of a product. We now look at three commonly used *non-model* approaches to demand forecasting, before turning to three examples of demand forecasting models.

4.2 Intention surveys

One obvious way of forecasting how many people will buy a home computer during the next six months might be to ask them! So we might do an *intention survey* to provide forecasts for a number of household goods.

Of course all surveys suffer from two major problems:

1. Can we be sure we have asked a representative sample of the population? We usually deal with this by:

Either making the sample as *random* as possible

or by making sure we get a carefully controlled cross-section of the population. This latter approach is the one used by the opinion polls featured in the press and on TV. They make sure they have a *quota* of each different kind of person in the population in their sample.

2. Can we be sure that the replies are trustworthy? Will people really go out and buy the items they have said? Again, there is a way of solving this problem: not to ask people questions which are

too specific or too far in the future. People can generally be trusted if they tell you they intend to buy a TV in the next three months. They cannot generally be trusted if they tell you they will buy a Sony TV in a year's time.

4.3 Summarizing survey answers

There are large programs for analysing surveys, but we can write a small one to total the answers to individual questions. First we show the output and then the program.

```
Totalling replies to a survey

How many questionnaires ?5

Question number ?22

Questionnaire No.1 Reply is ?0
Questionnaire No.2 Reply is ?2
Questionnaire No.3 Reply is ?1
Questionnaire No.4 Reply is ?2
Questionnaire No.5 Reply is ?0

Totals for Question number 22

        Code      Replies

         0           2
         1           1
         2           2
         3           0
         4           0
         5           0
         6           0
         7           0
         8           0
         9           0

A total of 5 Questionnaires
```

The program assumes that answers will have been coded 0 for no reply/do not know, and coded 1–9 for up to 9 possible answers.

```
90   DIM T(10)
100  FOR R = 1 TO 10
110  T(R) = 0
120  NEXT R
130  PRINT "Totalling replies to a survey"
140  PRINT

210  PRINT "How many questionnaires ";
220  INPUT N
230  PRINT
240  PRINT "Question number ";
250  INPUT Q
260  PRINT
265  FOR J = 1 TO N
270  PRINT "Questionnaire No. ";J;" Reply is ";
280  INPUT R
285  T(R+1) = T(R+1) + 1
290  NEXT J
```

```
510 PRINT
520 PRINT "Totals for Question number ";Q
530 PRINT
540 PRINT "        Code      Replies"
550 PRINT
560 FOR R = 1 TO 10
570 PRINT R-1,T(R)
580 NEXT R
585 PRINT
590 PRINT "A total of ";N;" Questionnaires"
```

4.4 Leading indicators

Demand for many products fluctuates, and it is difficult to predict when the upswings and downswings will take place. However we may be able to observe that the demand for some other product usually changes direction just before ours does. So we can use the other product as a *leading indicator* of what our product is likely to do.

This method is widely used in the UK and USA to forecast the upswings and downswings of the economy as a whole. Statisticians take a few products which usually change direction (say) six months before the rest of the economy, and combine them into a *six-month leading index*.

Our program LEADING does this:

```
90  DIM D(20), DIM W(20)
100 PRINT
110 PRINT "FORECASTING USING LEADING INDICATORS"
120 PRINT

210 PRINT "How many indicators ";
220 INPUT N
230 PRINT
240 PRINT "Please Input :"
250 PRINT
260 PRINT"Indicator  % Change  Weighting"
270 PRINT
275 FOR T = 1 TO N
280 PRINT TAB(4);T;TAB(12);
285 INPUT D(T)
287 PRINT TAB(24);
290 INPUT W(T)
295 NEXT T

310 FOR T = 1 TO N
320 OT = OT + D(T) * W(T)
330 W = W + W(T)
340 NEXT T
350 F = OT/W

510 PRINT
520 PRINT "From the indicators and weights above..."
530 PRINT "...the overall forecast is :"
540 PRINT
550 PRINT TAB(18);F;" %"
```

Of course, the leading program really only produces a weighted average of the components, but perhaps it is instructive to realize that the concept is as simple as that. In addition, the program can be used in any other situation where a number of indicators are combined to form another, such as a cost of living index.

With the leading indicators it may not be obvious which of the indicators to give extra weight to, and they may thus each receive a weight of 1. However, it is clear in the cost of living index that a change in the price of food should be given twice the weight of a change in the price of clothing if people, on average, spend twice as much of their income on food as on clothing.

4.5 Time series analysis

Our third example of a non-model approach to forecasting is the most important – Time Series Analysis. Anything which has been recorded for successive time periods is a time series, and time series analysis attempts to extract as much information as possible from the data itself.

One way of doing this is to fit curves to the existing data and then project (or *extrapolate*) these curves into the future.

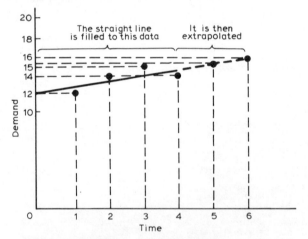

Figure 4.1 Projecting a straight line to forecast a time series

Computer programs to analyse time series can be very complex, but they all have one thing in common. They can only use the data of the time series itself, they do not have a model of why demand has changed, they can only say how it has changed.

Can we produce a program which will perform a simple time series analysis? We can, provided we are willing to make do with a straight line.

The technique of fitting a straight line to data is called *linear regression* and the *line of best fit* is defined as the one where the sum of the squares of the errors is minimized. Figure 4.2 may make this last sentence a little clearer.

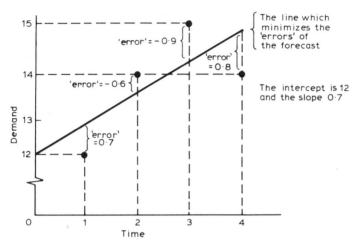

Figure 4.2 Linear regression – line of best fit

So the line shown is the one where the forecast (the line) shows the smallest errors (differences) from the actual data. (Why the differences are squared is explained in statistics and managerial economics books but is not crucial here.)

The actual formula for the straight line is a little complicated, but well worth the trouble. It is amazing how far we can get in economics or business with a straight line.

We need to know two *parameters* to specify a particular straight line:

the *intercept* and
the *slope*

(for a recap on the equation of a straight line see page 00.)

The intercept is

$$\frac{(\Sigma(x^2) * \Sigma y) - (\Sigma x - \Sigma xy)}{Z}$$

The slope is

$$\frac{N * \Sigma xy - \Sigma x * \Sigma y}{Z}$$

and Z is

$$N * \Sigma(x^2) - (\Sigma x)^2$$

Where: N is the number of observations
         x is the value on the horizontal axis
         y is the value on the vertical axis

So:

term above	means	Program variable
Σx	the sum of the x values	TX
Σy	the sum of the y values	TY
Σxy	the sum of all the $x * y$ values	TT
$\Sigma(x^2)$	the sum of all x^2	X2

The program LINFORC looks like this:

```
90   DIM D(20)
100  PRINT
110  PRINT "FORECASTING USING A STRAIGHT LINE"
120  PRINT

210  PRINT "How many observations ";
220  INPUT N
230  PRINT
240  PRINT "Please Input :"
250  PRINT
260  FOR T = 1 TO N
270  PRINT "Observation ";T;" ";
280  PRINT INPUT D(T)
290  NEXT T

310  FOR T = 1 TO N
320  TX = TX + T
330  TY = TY + D(T)
340  X2 = X2 + T^2
350  TT = TT + T * D(T)
360  NEXT T

399  REM *** CALCULATE SLOPE & INTERCEPT ***
400  Z = N * X2 - TX^2
410  B = (N * TT - TX * TY) / Z
420  A = (X2 * TY - TX * TT) / Z

510  PRINT
520  PRINT "The Intercept is ";A
530  PRINT
540  PRINT "and the Slope is ";B
550  PRINT
560  PRINT "How many periods ahead ";
565  INPUT F
570  M = N + F
575  FOR T = N + 1 TO M
580  PRINT
585  D = A + B * T
590  PRINT "Forecast for Period ";T;" : ";D
595  NEXT T
```

If we run the program we should get the following output.

```
>RUN

FORECASTING USING A STRAIGHT LINE

How many observations ?4

Please input :

Observation 1 ?12
Observation 2 ?14
Observation 3 ?15
Observation 4 ?14

The Intercept is 12

and the Slope is 0.7

How many periods ahead ?2

Forecast for Period 5 : 15.5
Forecast for Period 6 : 16.2

Ready
```

So we now have a simple but versatile program which can be used to fit straight lines to demand, or indeed any other, data.

Using it with some obviously curved data should demonstrate the dangers in using straight lines for forecasting.

For instance, consider the data for oil production in the UK:

1975	1.4 M tonnes
1976	11.8
1977	37.5
1978	53.3
1979	77.9
1980	80.5
1981	89.4
1982	103.4
1983	114.9

If we use our program to fit a straight line to this data, we get the prediction that oil production will keep on rising for ever! However, we know that this cannot be true and that UK oil production is now at or near its peak, and should decline gradually over the next few years.

In other words we have information outside the time series which will help us to forecast its future pattern. It is this outside or *a priori* information which is the basis of all models of demand, and it is to model-based forecasting that we now turn.

4.6 Income-based forecasts

One of the strongest predictors of people's buying habits is their income. Rich people spend more than poor people on almost everything, for obvious reasons, and people spend more as their incomes go up.

We can use an adaptation of our previous program to fit a straight line to the relationship between income and demand. For instance, we could use the national income of a country, and the demand for electricity.

We can take the LINFORC program and add the following lines:

```
95  DIM Y(20)
120 PRINT "RELATIONSHIP BETWEEN INCOME AND DEMAND"
130 PRINT

260 PRINT "Observation   Income      Demand"
270 PRINT
275 FOR T = 1 TO N
280 PRINT TAB(4);T;TAB(12);
285 INPUT Y(T)
287 PRINT TAB(24);
290 INPUT D(T)
295 NEXT T

320 TX = TX + Y(T)
340 X2 = X2 + Y(T)^2
350 TT = TT + Y(T) * D(T)

560 PRINT "... and so Demand changes ";B
570 PRINT "for every 1 increase in Income"
585 PRINT "... and Demand would be ";A
590 PRINT "at an income of 0"
595 PRINT
```

The output from the program should be:

```
FORECASTING USING A STRAIGHT LINE
RELATIONSHIP BETWEEN INCOME AND DEMAND

How many observations ?3

Please Input :

Observation   Income      Demand

     1         ?600
                           ?150
     2         ?650
                           ?162.5
     3         ?700
                           ?175

The Intercept is 0

and the Slope is 0.25

...and so Demand changes 0.25
for every 1 increase in Income

...and the Demand would be 0
at an Income of 0
```

The complete program is now:

```
90  DIM D(20)
95 DIM Y(20)
100 PRINT
110 PRINT "FORECASTING USING A STRAIGHT LINE"
120 PRINT "RELATIONSHIP BETWEEN INCOME AND DEMAND"
130 PRINT

210 PRINT "How many observations ";
220 INPUT N
230 PRINT
240 PRINT "Please Input :"
250 PRINT
260 PRINT "Observation   Income     Demand"
270 PRINT
275 FOR T = 1 TO N
280 PRINT TAB(4);T;TAB(12);
285 INPUT Y(T)
287 PRINT TAB(24);
290 INPUT D(T)
295 NEXT T

310 FOR T = 1 TO N
320 TX = TX + Y(T)
330 TY = TY + D(T)
340 X2 = X2 + Y(T)^2
350 TT = TT + Y(T) * D(T)
360 NEXT T

399 REM *** CALCULATE SLOPE & INTERCEPT ***
400 Z = N * X2 - TX^2
410 B = (N * TT - TX * TY) / Z
420 A = (X2 * TY - TX * TT) / Z

510 PRINT
520 PRINT "The Intercept is ";A
530 PRINT
540 PRINT "and the Slope is ";B
550 PRINT
560 PRINT "...and so Demand changes ";B
570 PRINT "for every 1 increase in Income"
580 PRINT
585 PRINT "...and Demand would be ";A
590 PRINT "at an income of 0"
595 PRINT
```

4.7 Income elasticity of demand

As we saw in Chapter 3, we often find that the relationship between changes in income and changes in demand is of the elasticity type rather than the linear one used above.

There are two ways we can deal with this:

1. Using the logarithms of data

If we use the logarithms of the data, the answers supplied by the program are no longer the intercept and slope, but they are the constant (A) and the income elasticity (B) in the following equation:

$$D = A * Y \uparrow B$$

and if you want to use the previous program in this way you should change the program as follows:

```
110 PRINT "FORECASTING USING AN ELASTICITY"

260 PRINT "Observation LogIncome LogDemand"

520 PRINT "The constant is ";A
540 PRINT "and the Income Elasticity is ";B
560 PRINT "...and so Demand changes ";B;" %"
570 PRINT "for every 1 % increase in Income"
585
590
595
```

2. Using income elasticity directly

We can often use other people's surveys to obtain a figure for IED (income elasticity of demand). For instance, in some countries the Agriculture Ministry has figures for foods in common consumption such as meat, bread and milk.

We can then write a very short program to use IED to forecast future demand, assuming, of course, that we also have a forecast of future income!

We can call our program ELASINC:

```
100 PRINT
110 PRINT "FORECASTING USING INCOME ELASTICITY"
120 PRINT

210 PRINT "I E D please ";
220 INPUT I
230 PRINT
240 PRINT "Income Now ";
250 INPUT Y1
260 PRINT
270 PRINT "Income next year ";
280 INPUT Y2
285 PRINT
290 PRINT "Demand this year ";
295 INPUT D1

310 Y9 = Y2 / Y1
320 D9 = Y9 * I
330 D2 = D1 * D9

510 PRINT
520 PRINT "If Income changes from ";y1;" to ";y2
530 PRINT "... and I E D is ";I
540 PRINT
550 PRINT "Demand should change from ";D1;" to ";D2
```

4.8 Using price and income elasticities

Of course it is much better if we have information on both PED (price elasticity of demand) and IED. This is particularly important if PED is significant and/or if large price changes are likely to take place.

An extreme recent example has been the changes in the price of fuels in the 1970s which revealed that PED was quite high for some fuels as soon as people had a chance to change their buying habits.

If we leave this question of the speed of response aside (it is very difficult to model), we can add to our previous IED program the following lines:

```
110 PRINT "FORECASTING USING PED AND IED"

201 PRINT "P E D please ";
202 INPUT P
203 PRINT
204 PRINT "Price this year ";
205 INPUT P1
206 PRINT
207 PRINT "Price next year ";
208 INPUT P2
209 PRINT

324 P9 = P2 / P1
326 D8 = P9 * P
330 D2 = D1 * D9 * D8

512 PRINT "If Price changes from ";P1;" to ";P2
514 PRINT "...and PED is ";P
516 PRINT
```

All we need now, of course, are forecasts of price and income changes!

Is this where we started?

4.9 Conclusion

There are a wide variety of methods of forecasting demand, and the one that we choose depends on the amount of time (and money) that we have available, the accuracy of the result that we want, and the kind of data that we can get to work on.

Further reading

There are an enormous number of books on demand forecasting. A gentle introduction might be chapters from:

RANDALL, K., *Managerial Economics*, London: Heinemann Educational Books, 1982
WAGNER, L. and BALTAZZIS, N., *Readings in Applied Microeconomics*. Oxford: Clarendon Press and The Open University, 1973

EXERCISES

(4.1) Use the *Annual Abstract of Statistics* to obtain data about the sales of a product for ten years.

Use the data for the first five years to forecast the sales for the last five years.

Check your results with the actual sales and comment on the accuracy, or otherwise, of your prediction.

(4.2) Use the *Annual Abstract* again to find five years' data on national Income and the sales of a product.

Find a relationship between National Income and the sales of the product.

Using the National Income figure for another year, forecast the sales of the product.

Comment on the accuracy, or otherwise, of your results.

(4.3) Obtain data for another country and repeat exercises 1 and 2. Suitable sources are:

The United Nations Statistical Yearbook
The OECD Observer
The European Community Statistical Handbook

Chapter 5

Supply and the firm

5.1 Production functions and cost curves

When we look at the producing side of a firm we are mainly
interested in two things:

The *Production function*: what happens to output when we
increase the number of workers, materials and so on.

The *Cost curves*: how costs change as we increase output.

They are connected by the price we have to pay for materials, and
the wages we have to pay workers. In fact, once we know the costs
per unit of the *inputs* (materials and workers) and the production
function we can work out the cost curves.

We now see how this can be done for two different kinds of
production function.

5.2 A linear production function

In some situations we can double the output by doubling the
numbers of workers and material. If this relationship holds over a
range of inputs we would term it *linear*. That is, it can be
represented by a straight line on a graph.

So a linear production function would show an increase in
output which was proportional to the increase in inputs.

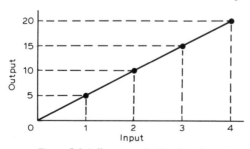

Figure 5.1 A linear production function

What would the cost curves look like? It is tempting to assume that they would all be linear as well. Certainly the *total cost* would rise in a straight line as output rose, if wages and material costs remained the same per unit. (Doubling output would require a doubling of workers and materials and this would double their total cost.)

However, there would be some other costs as well as wages and materials. These other costs do not vary with output and are thus often called *fixed* costs or overheads. This is to contrast them with the costs which vary with output which are termed *variable* costs.

So, as output rose, the variable costs would rise but the *average* variable costs would remain the same. The fixed costs would remain the same but the average fixed costs would fall as they were shared between more units of output.

A very short program will illustrate this:

```
100 PRINT
110 PRINT "FIXED AND VARIABLE COSTS"
120 PRINT

200 PRINT "Fixed Cost please ";
210 INPUT F
220 PRINT
230 PRINT "Variable cost per unit please ";
240 INPUT V
250 PRINT

510 PRINT "        Fixed  Variable  Total   Average"
520 PRINT "Output  Costs   Costs    Costs    Costs"
530 PRINT
540 FOR Q = 1 TO 10
550 T = F + V * Q
560 A = (INT(T*100/Q+0.5))/100
570 PRINT TAB(2);Q;TAB(9);F;TAB(17);V*Q;TAB(25);T;TAB(32);A
580 NEXT Q
```

The output from the program should be:

```
FIXED AND VARIABLE COSTS

Fixed costs please ?100

Variable cost per unit please ?10
```

Output	Fixed Costs	Variable Costs	Total Costs	Average Costs
1	100	10	110	110
2	100	20	120	60
3	100	30	130	43.33
4	100	40	140	35
5	100	50	150	30
6	100	60	160	26.66
7	100	70	170	24.28
8	100	80	180	22.5
9	100	90	190	21.11
10	100	100	200	20

So we see that although the fixed, variable and total costs are linear, the average costs are curved. Graph the average cost against output if you are not convinced.

You could see the cause, if you ran the program with fixed cost at 100 and variable cost per unit at 0. This would show that the average fixed cost is the cause of the curved shape of the average cost curve. Average fixed costs decline very steeply at first, and then more and more slowly.

5.3 A marginalist production function

The output of some products responds to additional inputs in a non-linear way, with the output going up by less each time an input is increased.

We call the extra output the marginal productivity of the input that caused it, and we say that the input has *diminishing marginal productivity* or that there are *diminishing returns* to the input being varied.

We can illustrate this with another short program:

```
90   DIM Q(6),L(6)
100  Q(0) = 0
110  L(0) = 0

210  PRINT
220  PRINT "A MARGINALIST PRODUCTION FUNCTION"
230  PRINT " - DIMINISHING RETURNS TO AN INPUT"
240  PRINT
250  PRINT "Number of machines please ";
260  INPUT K
270  PRINT

510  PRINT "Number of   Number of   Total    Marginal"
520  PRINT "Machines    Workers     Output   Product"
530  PRINT
540  FOR T = 1 TO 5
545  PRINT TAB(2);K;TAB(12);
550  INPUT L(T)
555  Q(T) = K^.5 * L(T)^.5
560  Q(T) = (INT(Q*10+0.5))/10
565  CQ = Q(T)-Q(T-1)
570  CL = L(T)-L(T-1)
575  MP = CQ / CL
580  MP = (INT(MP*10+0.5))/10
585  PRINT TAB(23);Q(T);TAB(31);MP
587  PRINT "-------------------------------------"
590  NEXT T
```

The output from the program might be:

```
A MARGINALIST PRODUCTION FUNCTION
 - DIMINISHING RETURNS TO AN INPUT

Number of machines please ?100

Number of    Number of    Total    Marginal
Machines     Workers      Output   Product

   100          ?1
                           10       10
------------------------------------------------
   100          ?2
                           14.1     4.1
------------------------------------------------
   100          ?3
                           17.3     3.2
------------------------------------------------
   100          ?4
                           20       2.7
------------------------------------------------
   100          ?5
                           22.3     2.3
------------------------------------------------
```

We now wish to change our production function into a cost function, and this entails calculating the marginal cost (cost of an extra unit of output). We obtain an approximate value for this by dividing the change in cost by the change in output. The changes to the previous program are:

```
90   DIM Q(6),L(6),C(6)

230 PRINT " - CALCULATING MARGINAL COST"
265 PRINT
270 PRINT "Cost per machine please ";
275 INPUT R
277 C(0) = K * R
280 PRINT
285 PRINT "Cost per worker please ";
290 INPUT W
295 PRINT

510 PRINT"                          Total Marginal"
520 PRINT"Machines Workers Output   Costs Cost"
563 C(T) = K*R + L(T)*W
570 CC = C(T) - C(T-1)
575 MC = CC / CQ
580 MC = (INT(MC*10+0.5))/10
585 PRINT TAB(18);Q(T);TAB(25);C(T);TAB(32);MC
```

In this program C(T) is the total cost, made up of the machinery cost (K * R) and the labour cost (L(T) * W).

CC is the change in total cost when the number of workers changes, and we calculate it by taking the previous cost (C(T−1)) from the present cost (C(T)).

We have to make an assumption about the cost with 0 workers and the most reasonable one seems to be that there will be just the fixed cost of the machinery, and this is calculated at line 277.

CQ is the change in output and so marginal cost is CC/CQ.

With some carefully chosen costs we can see clearly that a function which has diminishing returns (we have not changed the production function in the program) will also show increasing marginal cost.

The output from the program should be:

```
A MARGINALIST PRODUCTION FUNCTION
 - CALCULATING MARGINAL COST

Number of machines please ?100

Cost per machine please ?2

Cost per worker please ?20

                          Total  Marginal
Machines Workers Output   Costs  Cost

   100      ?1
                   10      220    2
  _____
   100      ?2
                   14.1    240    4.8
  _____
   100      ?3
                   17.3    260    6.2
  _____
   100      ?4
                   20      280    7.4
  _____
   100      ?5
                   22.3    300    8.6
  _____
```

So the marginal cost rises as more workers are used with the same number of machines, not because the cost per worker increases, but because there is diminishing returns to labour.

Of course there are also diminishing returns to machinery with this production function, and you could try to change the program to demonstrate this.

5.4 Revenue curves

The other side of the firm that we are interested in of course is its revenue.

We can classify firms as either *price-takers* or *price-makers*.

A price-taker has to accept whatever price exists, either because the price is set by the market or perhaps because it is controlled in some way.

A price-maker however can control the price, but of course cannot control the customers! This means that price has to be lower in order to sell more, so the price (*average revenue*) falls as sales increase.

However, the price has to be reduced on all units sold, so if we lower price by 1p to increase sales by ten units we lose 1p on all the other units we sell as well. This effect is recorded by the *marginal revenue*, which we can express arithmetically as:

$$\text{Marginal revenue} = \frac{\text{change in total revenue}}{\text{change in sales}}$$

We will now write a program which puts together the diminishing returns production function and the downward sloping demand curve facing a price-maker.

5.5 A profit-maximizing model of the firm

If a firm is trying to maximize its profits it will look at each increase in output to see if it adds more to revenue than to cost. That is, is *marginal revenue* greater than *marginal cost*. It is profitable to expand production as long as this occurs.

Our program lets us find out how far to expand output.

We input two different outputs, preferably close together and the program calculates the profit at each output and the marginal cost and marginal revenue caused by the output change.

We use READ . . . DATA to set up the values for the model. The program is:

```
 90  DIM Q(2),C(2),D(2),P(2),R(2),X(2)

100  READ K,R
110  READ W
120  READ A,B

210  PRINT
220  PRINT "First output/sales please ";
230  INPUT Q(1)
240  PRINT
250  PRINT "Second output/sales please ";
260  INPUT Q(2)
270  PRINT

310  FOR T= 1 TO 2
320  L = (Q(T)/K^.5)^2
330  C(T) = K*R + L*W
340  P(T) = (Q(T)-A)/B
350  R(T) = Q(T) * P(T)
355  X(T) = R(T)-C(T)
360  NEXT T
370  CR = R(2)-R(1)
375  CC = C(2)-C(1)
380  CQ = Q(2)-Q(1)
385  MR = CR / CQ
390  MC = CC / CQ

510  PRINT
520  PRINT "                        First      Second"
525  PRINT
530  PRINT "Output";TAB(20);Q(1);TAB(30);Q(2)
535  PRINT "Total Cost";TAB(20);C(1);TAB(30);C(2)
540  PRINT
```

```
545 PRINT "Sales";TAB(20);Q(1);TAB(30);Q(2)
550 PRINT "Price";TAB(20);P(1);TAB(30);P(2)
555 PRINT "Total Revenue";TAB(20);R(1);TAB(30);R(2)
560 PRINT
565 PRINT "Profit";TAB(20);X(1);TAB(30);X(2)
570 PRINT
575 PRINT "Change in Revenue";TAB(25);CR
580 PRINT "Change in Sales";TAB(25);CQ
585 PRINT
590 PRINT "MARGINAL REVENUE";TAB(25);MR
595 PRINT
600 PRINT "MARGINAL COST";TAB(25);MC

3000 DATA 100,2
3010 DATA 20
3020 DATA 50,-2
```

The results should be something like:

```
First output/sales please ?14

Second output/sales please ?16

                          First      Second

Output                    14         16
Total Cost                239.2      251.2

Sales                     14         16
Price                     18         17
Total Revenue             252        272

Profit                    12.8       20.8

Change in Revenue              20
Change in Sales                2

MARGINAL REVENUE               10

MARGINAL COST                  6
```

At these outputs we still seem to be in a position where marginal revenue is greater than marginal cost. So it would be sensible to increase output. Perhaps you would like to check the output at which profits are maximized.

At some outputs some of the figures will be printed to several decimal places. To keep the program easy to read we did not include our usual method of rounding to (say) 2 decimal places. Again, you could do this if you wish.

5.6 A linear model of the firm

A simple linear model of the firm which is often used by accountants, and increasingly by economists is the *break even* model.

The firm is faced with a constant price for its product (in the profit-maximizing jargon it is a price-taker). Its costs divide into fixed and variable costs exactly as we discussed in section 5.2.

These costs and revenue assumptions can be shown in a break-even chart (Figure 5.2).

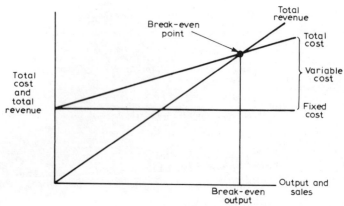

Figure 5.2 Break-even chart

So the revenue goes up as sales go up, and if the price per unit (average revenue) is greater than the variable cost per unit (average variable cost) each unit sold will make some contribution to the fixed costs. The point where the fixed costs have all been paid for is called the break-even point.

We could take our Fixed and Variable Costs program and add some lines to make it into a break-even program:

```
110 PRINT "BREAK-EVEN MODEL"
260 PRINT "Price per unit please ";
270 INPUT R
280 PRINT

510 PRINT"        Average  Average"
520 PRINT"Output   Cost     Revenue      Profit"
570 P = (R-A) * Q
575 P = (INT(P*10+0.5))/10
580 PRINT TAB(2);Q;TAB(10);A;TAB(20);R;TAB(30);P
590 NEXT Q
```

The output should look like this:

```
BREAK-EVEN MODEL

Fixed costs please ?100

Variable cost per unit please ?10

Price per unit please ?22

         Average  Average
Output   Costs    Revenue   Profit

   1      110       22       -88
   2      60        22       -76
   3      43.33     22       -64
   4      35        22       -52
   5      30        22       -40
   6      26.67     22       -28
   7      24.29     22       -16
   8      22.5      22       -4
   9      21.11     22        8
  10      20        22        20
```

So our firm breaks even at an output of between 8 and 9 units. At present the program only looks at outputs between 0 and 10, but you should be able to change that quite easily.

An obvious question to ask about our break-even model is when to stop increasing output! Every time we increase output by 1 unit the marginal cost is 10 and the marginal revenue is 22 so we always add 12 to profit.

There are two answers:

1. There will always be some limit either to what the customers will buy, or on the size of the factory or the number of people we can get to work for us. These are what will stop us increasing output for ever.

2. Break-even models are meant to be used to find out the minimum level of output we need in order to break-even, and so the simple (linear) assumptions of constant price and variable costs are useful simplifications. If we wanted to consider the *best* output we should probably have to use a more complicated model. Our profit-maximizing model might be suitable, or we might use linear-programming which is a bit too complicated for this book.

5.7 Conclusion

There are a variety of models that can be used to understand and control firms, and we use the one which fits our needs and the amount of time, money and data that we have available.

Further reading

Any economics or managerial economics text contains several chapters on models of the firm, or *theory of the firm* as economists often call it. A gentle introduction might be:

HAWKINS, C. J., *Theory of the Firm*. London: Macmillan, 1976.
RANDALL, K., *Managerial Economics*. London: Heinemann Educational Books, 1982

EXERCISES

(4.1) Obtain data for an industry's output and costs from the *Annual Abstract of Statistics* and use the line fitting program from Chapter 4 to find the intercept and slope of the total cost function.

Use this to forecast its costs at other outputs.

Have you found the industry's fixed and variable costs?

(4.2) Use the graph subroutine to produce graphs of the different cost curves from both the linear and marginalist production functions. Are they what you expected?

(4.3) Re-arrange the marginalist model to show diminishing returns to machines.

(4.4) Re-arrange the program again so that you can choose to vary both machinery and workers.
    Increase both equally and note what happens to output.

$$\frac{\% \text{ change in output}}{\% \text{ change in all inputs}}$$ is called the *returns to scale*.

Check in one of the texts in the further reading above what it means if there is increasing/constant/decreasing returns to scale.

(4.5) Amend the profit-maximizing program so that it tells you when you have reached the profit-maximizing output.

(4.6) Amend the break-even program so that it tells you what the break-even output would be.

Chapter 6

Investment appraisal

6.1 What is investment?

In everyday language we use the term investment for buying something which will either increase in value or give us some kind of income. So we speak of investing in a house, or a building society. Businesses invest in machinery, vehicles and the shares of other companies. What all these 'investments' involve is committing your money to some use for a period of time in the hope that it will benefit you in some way. So it involves comparing the benefit of spending the money now with the benefits that will come from the investment.

We can see that investment really involves two different problems:

1. Is it better to have benefits now or in the future? (Is it worth investing at all?)
2. Which investment opportunity should we take?

People have always found it easier to answer the second question so we shall start with it and come back to the first question in section 6.4.

6.2 The pay-back method of investment appraisal

If we decide to invest £500 in insulating our house, we might have three ways of spending it, each with its own effects on our heating bills.

Table 6.1

Project	Details	Cost	Saving on heating
A	Loft insulation and some double glazing	£500	£ 80 a year
B	Double-glazing only	£500	£100 a year
C	Cavity-wall foam insulation	£500	£110 a year

If we take only these money flows into account it seems obvious that it is better to undertake project C, the cavity-wall foam insulation. It saves more money each year for the same initial cost.

What if the initial costs were different? Let's take a closer look at project A. We find that the loft insulation costs £150 and saves £40 a year, while the double-glazing part of this project costs £350 and saves £40.

So, if we can just do the loft insulation on its own it looks more attractive than if it is combined with £350 worth of rather ineffective double-glazing.

One way of comparing it with the other projects is the *pay-back method*. We calculate how long an investment takes to pay back its cost.

Project B takes 5 years (£100 a year for five years)
Project C takes 4–5 years
Project A takes 6–7 years

But loft insulation alone pays back in 3–4 years, and some people would regard this as a better use of their money than the other projects.

Obviously, simple projects like our example can be calculated easily, but for more complicated numbers we could use a simple program.

First the program output:

```
PAY-BACK PERIOD

What is the cost of the Project ?100

How many inflows of cash are there ?4

Inflow during period 1 ?28
Inflow during period 2 ?25
Inflow during period 3 ?24
Inflow during period 4 ?29

This project pays back its cost
...during period 4
```

The program itself is quite simple:

```
90   DIM D(20)
100  PRINT
110  PRINT "PAY-BACK PERIOD"
120  PRINT

210  PRINT "What is the cost of the Project ";
220  INPUT C
230  PRINT
240  PRINT "How many inflows of cash are there ";
250  INPUT N
260  PRINT
```

```
270 FOR T = 1 TO N
280 PRINT "Inflow during period ";T;" ";
290 INPUT D(T)
295 NEXT T

310 FOR T = 1 TO N
320 IN = IN + D(T)
330 IF IN >= C THEN 510
340 NEXT T
350 PRINT
360 PRINT "This project has NOT paid for itself"
370 PRINT "...by period ";N
380 GOTO 999

510 PRINT
520 PRINT "This project pays back its cost"
530 IF IN = C THEN 560
540 PRINT "...during period ";T
550 GOTO 999
560 PRINT "...in exactly ";T;" time periods"

999 END
```

So using our payback program could help us to decide which kind
of insulation was best at getting our money back quickly.

6.3 Average return on capital

However, using the payback approach does imply that we want a
quick return on our money rather than the best return in the long
run. What if the costs and returns looked like Figure 6.1?

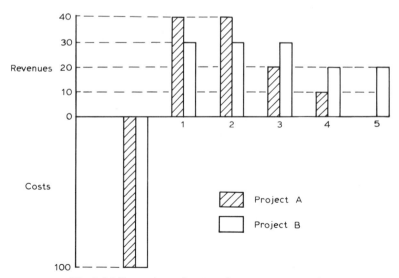

Figure 6.1 Comparison of costs and returns on two projects

We see that project A pays back *soonest*, in three years, but that project B pays back *more* over five years. Over the five years project A brings in 10 more than it costs, while project B brings in 30 more than it costs.

There are two ways of calculating the *average return on capital*:

1. Average gross return $= \dfrac{\text{gross inflow } \%}{\text{Number of years}}$

2. Average net return $= \dfrac{\text{net inflow } \%}{\text{Number of years}}$

In the gross case we ignore the cost and divide the inflow by the number of years, giving:

110/5 = 22% for project A
130/5 = 26% for project B

This leaves both projects looking good, with B slightly better.
In the net case we take off the cost giving:

10/5 = 2% for project A
30/5 = 6% for project B

B is still better, but the gap now looks wider.
A program to calculate the average rate of return would be very simple:

```
 90  DIM D(20)
100  PRINT
110  PRINT "AVERAGE RATE OF RETURN"
120  PRINT

210  PRINT "What is the cost of the Project ";
220  INPUT C
230  PRINT
240  PRINT "How many inflows of cash are there ";
250  INPUT N
260  PRINT
270  FOR T = 1 TO N
280  PRINT "Inflow during period ";T;" ";
290  INPUT D(T)
295  NEXT T

310  FOR T = 1 TO N
320  IN = IN + D(T)
330  NEXT T
340  P = 100 / C
350  G = (IN / T) * P
360  N = ((IN - C)/T) / C

510  PRINT
520  PRINT "The average GROSS return is ";G;" %"
530  PRINT
540  PRINT "and the average NET return is ";N;" %"
```

and a typical output from the program would be:

```
AVERAGE RATE OF RETURN

What is the cost of the Project ?200

How many inflows of cash are there ?2

Inflow during period 1 ?120
Inflow during period 2 ?100

The average GROSS return is 55 %

and the average NET return is 5 %
```

So the average rate of return method looks at the whole life of a project rather than just seeing which project pays for itself soonest.

So should we prefer the technique which concentrates on when returns occur (payback), or the one which concentrates on their total value (average rate of return)?

Ideally we need a technique which does both. This brings us to the discounting approach.

6.4 Discounting

Most of us are familiar with the idea of *compound interest*. If we leave money in the Building Society it grows at a 'compound' rate, that is it appears to grow faster as time passes. This is because the interest on the first year's investment is left in to earn interest itself and so on.

We could construct a table of the value of, say £100, at intervals of a year.

Table 6.2

Time from now (years)	Value in pounds
0	100
1	110
2	121
3	133.1

The rate of interest in this case being 10%.

We now need some technical terms in which to describe what we are doing. If we call the amount invested the *principal*, and know the rate of (compound) interest which we can obtain we can describe 133.1 as the *future value* in 3 years of 100 invested at 10%.

Alternatively, 121 is the future value in 2 years of 100 invested at 10%.

Extending the idea, the *present value* of 121 in 2 years' time if the interest rate is 10% is 100.

So we can summarize the concepts of present and future value in the following diagram.

```
PRESENT              COMPOUND              FUTURE
VALUE   >>>>>>>>  INTEREST  >>>>>>>>   VALUE


PRESENT                                FUTURE
VALUE   <<<<<<<<      ?      <<<<<<<<   VALUE
```

What is the equivalent of the interest rate when going backwards in time? It is the rate of *discount*. So to find the present value of some future sum we can use the rate of discount.

The next problem is: 'How can we do the calculations easily?' Obviously we could use a computer program which did the calculation for each year in turn, going forwards or backwards as the case might be.

Another, easier, method is to use a formula which summarizes the process. For compound interest we have the formula:

$$\text{FUTURE VALUE} = \text{PRESENT VALUE} * (1 + r)^t$$

where

r is the interest rate expressed as a decimal (for instance, 10% is expressed as 0.10)

t is the year number
(2 means 2 years from the present)

Going backwards in time, the formula becomes:

$$\text{PRESENT VALUE} = \text{FUTURE VALUE} * \frac{1}{(1+r)^t}$$

So one formula is the reciprocal (mirror-image) of the other.
We can now produce a simple discounting program.

```
 90  DIM C(20),D(20),P(20)
100  PRINT
110  PRINT "DISCOUNTING CASH FLOWS"
120  PRINT

210  PRINT "What is the cost of the Project ";
220  INPUT C
230  PRINT
240  PRINT "How many inflows of cash are there ";
```

```
250 INPUT N
255 PRINT
260 FOR T = 1 TO N
265 PRINT "Inflow during period ";T;" "
270 INPUT D(T)
275 NEXT T
280 PRINT
285 PRINT "Discount Rate (%) please ";
290 INPUT R
295 R = R/100

310 G = 0
320 N = 0
330 FOR T = 1 TO N
340 D(T) = 1 / (1+R)^T
350 P(T) = C(T) * D(T)
360 G = G + P(T)
370 NEXT T
380 N = G - C

510 PRINT
520 PRINT "The GROSS Present Value is ";G
530 PRINT
540 PRINT "and the NET Present Value is ";N
```

Using the cash flows from project A in section 6.3, we get the following output.

```
DISCOUNTING CASH FLOWS

What is the cost of the Project ?100

How many inflows of cash are there ?4

Inflow during period 1 ?40
Inflow during period 2 ?40
Inflow during period 3 ?20
Inflow during period 4 ?10

Discount Rate (%) please ?5

The GROSS Present Value is 99.93

and the NET Present Value is -0.07
```

You are probably now asking: 'What does discounting actually do – what kind of projects will be chosen?'

We can answer this by looking at a famous example (Henderson, 1971) which discounts the cash flows from six projects.

Table 6.3 Cash flows for six projects

Project	0	1	2	3	4	5
			Cash flows in each year			
A	−100	100	10	–	–	–
B	−100	50	50	10	10	–
C	−100	40	30	30	20	10
D	−100	28	28	28	28	28
E	−100	10	20	30	40	50
F	−100	–	–	–	40	120

The object is to decide which project is the best, assuming we can only invest 100.

We could use the payback method, putting them in the order in which they pay back the 100 invested. This gives the order A, B, C, D, E, F.

If we used the average return method we could calculate:

Table 6.4

Project	Average gross return (%)	Average net return (%)
A	22	2
B	24	4
C	26	6
D	28	8
E	30	10
F	32	12

Giving the order of preference F, E, D, C, B, A.

So, as we might expect, the non-discounting techniques give opposite answers.

If we now use our program to discount each project's cash flows at 8% we get the following results:

Table 6.5

Project	Net present value
A	1.2
B	4.5
C	8.0
D	11.8
E	13.6
F	11.1

So discounting suggests the order: E, D, F, C, B, A.

However, what if we used a different discount rate?

If we used 2.5% we would get the following results:

Table 6.6

Project	Net present value
A	7.1
B	14.8
C	22.4
D	30.1
E	37.1
F	42.3

and the order: F, E, D, C, B, A.

On the other hand, 15% would give:

Table 6.7

Project	Net present value
A	− 5.4
B	− 6.4
C	− 6.4
D	− 6.2
E	− 8.7
F	−17.4

and the order: A, D, B and C, E, F.

So the order in which projects appear after discounting depends on the rate of discount and not on discounting itself. A high rate of discount can give the same results as the payback method and a very low rate the same result as the average rate of return approach.

6.5 The internal rate of return

An obvious question to ask is why we have to express discounting results in terms of net present values. The short answer is that we can show the results of discounting in a different way, as a % return.

As we are discounting rather than averaging it is called the *internal rate of return* or IRR, and it is the rate of discount at which the NPV is 0. That is, the IRR is the rate of discount which the project can just survive. In some sense it is the discounted rate of return on the project. If we are presenting the results of discounting to people who are not familiar with discounting then the IRR, as a percentage, looks more familiar than the NPV. We can find the IRR by using our program with different discount rates until the NPV is 0.

To do so, add the following lines to the discounting program:

```
550 PRINT
560 PRINT "To use another discount rate type 1";
570 INPUT Q
580 IF Q = 1 THEN 280
```

However, there are some difficulties with using the IRR which are explained in managerial economics texts. The NPV, however, always represents the effect on the firm of making the investment. If it is positive it is the same as adding to the value of the company.

In a perfect world, undertaking this investment would add exactly the NPV to the value of the company's shares on the Stock Exchange.

The next obvious question is: 'What is the *correct* rate of discount?'

The answer will also tell us why we should invest at all – a question we asked at the beginning of the chapter.

6.6 Choosing the discount rate

When we discount future cash flows we give them a lower value than the same number of pounds now. Why? There are really two reasons: *opportunity cost* and *time preference*.

Our explanation of the mechanics of discounting was in terms of interest. At any one time we can obtain a particular rate of interest if we lend money and would have to pay a particular rate of interest if we borrowed. These rates are different but for large firms very close, say only 1% apart. For simplicity, let's average them and call them *the* rate of interest.

So, if we invest money in machinery we are giving up the chance of lending it at the present rate of interest. The *opportunity cost* of the investment is the rate of interest we could have obtained for the cash involved. So any of the cash flows will be discounted at this rate of interest (or discount). If interest rates go up the rate of discount used in investment appraisal should go up too.

However, there is another reason for discounting which is more individual in its origin. As individuals and as firms we have *time preference* – we prefer to use things now rather than in the future. We saw this clearly with the payback method; its users want their money back as soon as possible and this is the same as having a high rate of discount. Those using the average rate of return method valued £100 far off in the future the same as £100 now, and so really had a 0% discount rate.

Are these two approaches to choosing the discount rate likely to give different answers? They might, for instance if interest rates were high and a firm usually invested in projects with lower (discounted) rates of return. In this case the firm has to judge whether interest (opportunity cost) will fall soon, or whether it should cut back on its investments in machinery and factories for the present at least.

This helps to explain why firms do not build factories when interest rates are high; it is not just that some of them cannot repay the interest out of the cash flows from the project. Even those with money of their own find that it is better to lend money at the high interest rates than invest it in factories.

6.7 Summary

Putting money to work by investing in machinery and factories has to be compared with other uses of money. The best way to do this is to discount any cash flows which occur because of the project concerned – both outflows and inflows. The firm, or person, can then judge whether it is a good idea to invest at all, and which investment is best. Results may be easier to understand if they are in the form of the payback period or the internal rate of return, even though the NPV method has been used to calculate which is the best project.

Further reading

HENDERSON, P. D., 'Investment criteria for public enterprises' in *Public Enterprise*, Harmondsworth, Penguin Books, 1971 (an amended version of an article in *Bulletin of the Oxford University Institute of Economics and Statistics, Vol 27*, 1965, pp 55–89)

HAWKINS, C. J. and PEARCE, D. W., Capital Investment Appraisal. London: Macmillan, 1971

EXERCISES

(6.1) Use the IRR program to find the internal rate of return for each of the six projects in Section 6.4.

Is the ordering of the projects similar to that given by any of the other methods of investment appraisal? Why/why not?

(6.2) Change the discounting program so that it gives the following output:

YEAR   CASH FLOW   DISCOUNT FACTOR   PRESENT VALUE

....

etc.

Chapter 7
Keynesian macroeconomics

7.1 Introduction

Fifty years ago there occurred one of the most radical shifts in thinking about how market economies operate since the writings of Adam Smith in the late 18th century. When John Maynard Keynes published his 'General Theory of Employment, Interest and Money' in 1936 he produced a revolution in ideas and in policy. The 'Keynesian revolution' overturned decades of thinking which Keynes described as 'the classical view'. This view suggested that economies were self-regulating; that is, market forces could be relied upon to produce full employment without the assistance of governments. Keynes not only set out to show why these ideas were wrong and to replace them with an alternative model of the economy, but also provided a very practical guide to show how governments, by accepting a new policy responsibility, could reduce unemployment, and could maintain full employment once it was achieved. The economic and social consequences of mass unemployment of the 1930s created a climate in which these ideas were rapidly accepted, and for more than 30 years after the second world war they shaped government policy under both Conservative and Labour administrations.

This chapter examines the 'Keynesian revolution' and some of the problems involved in conducting a Keynesian policy, through a series of basic programs. This will introduce you to what is called 'macroeconomics'. As this branch of economics is different from those considered in earlier chapters, it will be useful to outline what is meant by the term.

Macroeconomics is concerned with aggregates. We attempt to explain the total level of employment in an economy, rather than the number of workers employed by a single firm or even an industry. In the same way, we are interested in total income, not the earnings of an individual, and we examine the price level of all goods and services (and its rate of change, that is, inflation), not the price of individual products. This means macroeconomics

78

studies some of the most important economic, social and political problems of our time, including unemployment, inflation and growth.

7.2 The classical view

The classical view was that market economies were self-regulating – they could be relied upon to produce full employment. On the face of it, this seems an unlikely outcome. The market economy is highly decentralized with millions of individuals deciding on their own expenditure and thousands of firms deciding what to produce and how many workers to employ. Why should all these diverse plans result in full employment?

To help you understand the classical position, imagine an economy where there is no foreign trade (that is, no imports and exports) and no government. The economy is divided into two groups: households, who own and supply factors of production, and firms, who employ factors and produce goods and services.

Now look at Figure 7.1. The dotted lines show the supply of factors from households to firms and the flow of goods and services from firms to households. These are real flows for which

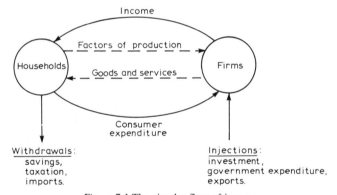

Figure 7.1 The circular flow of income

there are corresponding money flows, and we will concentrate on these. In return for supplying factors, households receive a money flow of income which consists of wages and salaries, interest payments, rents and profits. There is also a money flow of consumer expenditure from households to firms in payment for the goods and services they produce and supply to households. Thus we have a circular flow of income from one group or sector to another.

If all the income received by households were spent on the output of firms then there would be an equilibrium position – that is, from a macroeconomic viewpoint, the demand would exactly match the supply.

However, as Figure 7.1 shows, the position is likely to be more complicated. Some of the income will not be spent by households – it will be saved. This saving is represented as a withdrawal or leakage from the circular flow. But there is also an injection into the circular flow which results from investment expenditure. Economists use the term 'investment' to refer to expenditure on plant and machinery, and this provides a demand for output additional to that of households' consumer expenditure. If demand (by households and firms) is going to exactly match supply (the output produced by firms) then injections into the circular flow must be the same as withdrawals. In this case, equilibrium requires savings (withdrawals) and investment (injection) to be equal.

The classical economist believed that 'supply would create its own demand'; that is, there would always be sufficient demand to purchase the output produced by firms. This agreeable state of affairs would be produced because a market mechanism would ensure that savings and investment would always be equal. How did this work?

In the classical view all savings would be loaned. This would happen because it was assumed that people would prefer to receive a rate of interest on savings rather than receive nothing by keeping savings in the tea caddy or under the mattress. The volume of saving would be influenced by the level of income and the rate of interest. The higher the latter, the more would be saved.

Savings would be a supply of loanable funds, but who would borrow the money? In our simple economy the demand for loanable funds would come from investment expenditure because firms' spending on plant and machinery is in anticipation of future sales and requires financing in the short run. Firms would borrow more money and spend more on investment as the interest rate dropped.

The operation of the market for loanable funds ensures that savings and investment are equal and that there is always sufficient demand to buy output. Program 7.1 illustrates how this works. The program calculates and prints out an initial position where output and expenditure (consumption plus investment) are equal at 100. Investment and savings are both 35 and consumption expenditure, which is the difference between income and savings, is 65. The interest rate is 5%. You are given the option of shifting savings or investment. If you increase savings you will find the interest rate drops. Why is that?

Increased savings at the 5% interest rate means there is an excess supply of loanable funds because firms only wish to borrow 35. This excess supply drives the interest rate down which encourages investment and discourages some of the extra saving. Try various shifts of investment and savings and you will see that movements in the interest rate always keep them equal and that demand always matches output.

Program 7.1 Classical macro model

```
 10 REM PROGRAM  CLASSICAL A
 20 REM NO 7.1
 99 REM set fixed values
100 M$="INPUT NEW VALUE"
119 REM set initial values
120 READ A,B,C,D,G
130 READ J,H,S2,S3,I1
140 READ W1,Y
200 PRINT
299 REM calculations
400 S1=S2*Y
410 R = (I1-S1-S3)/(H-J)
420 I=I1+J*R
430 S=S3+S1+H*R
440 CN=Y-S
450 Z=CN+I
499 REM output results
500 PRINT
510 PRINT
520 PRINT"OUTPUT              = ";Y
530 PRINT"DEMAND              = ";Z
540 PRINT"CONSUMPTION         = ";CN
550 PRINT"INVESTMENT          = ";I
560 PRINT"SAVINGS             = ";S
570 PRINT"INTEREST RATE       = ";R
699 REM select option / input new values
700 PRINT
710 PRINT"**************"
720 PRINT"CHOOSE OPTION"
730 PRINT"**************"
740 PRINT
750 PRINT "1. END PROGRAM"
760 PRINT "2. SHIFT SAVING"
770 PRINT "3. SHIFT INVESTMENT"
790 INPUT R
800 IF R<1 OR R>3 THEN GOTO 790
810 IF R=1 THEN GOTO 990 : REM end
820 IF R=2 THEN GOSUB 1000 : REM shift saving
830 IF R=3 THEN GOSUB 1100 : REM shift investment
850 GOTO 200 : REM re-calculate
989 REM program end
990 PRINT"END OF PROGRAM"
995 END
998 REM subroutines
999 REM shift saving
1000 PRINT M$
1010 INPUT S4
1020 S3=S3+S4-S
1030 RETURN
```

```
1099 REM shift investment
1100 PRINT M$
1110 INPUT I2
1120 I1=I1+I2-I
1130 RETURN
2998 REM stored data
2999 REM initial values A,B,C,D,G
3000 DATA 50,-1,0,1,4
3009 REM J,H,S2,S3,I1
3010 DATA -5,5,.1,0,60
3019 REM W1,Y
3020 DATA 25,100
>RUN
```

```
OUTPUT                    = 100
DEMAND                    = 100
CONSUMPTION               = 65
INVESTMENT                = 35
SAVINGS                   = 35
INTEREST RATE             = 5

*************
CHOOSE OPTION
*************

1. END PROGRAM
2. SHIFT SAVING
3. SHIFT INVESTMENT
?2
INPUT NEW VALUE
?45
```

```
OUTPUT                    = 100
DEMAND                    = 100
CONSUMPTION               = 60
INVESTMENT                = 40
SAVINGS                   = 40
INTEREST RATE             = 4
```

One further aspect of the classical view needs examining. Whilst we have shown why 'supply always creates its own demand', we have not demonstrated that the level of output in the economy will be sufficiently high to give full employment. Another market mechanism will accomplish this task – the labour market. This market for workers, according to classical economists, can be regarded like any other market. There will be a demand for labour which depends on its price (that is, the wage rate): lower wages will encourage firms to take on more workers. The supply of labour will depend on wage rates, with higher wages attracting more workers to offer themselves for jobs. If there is unemployment, then in the classical view this is a result of wages being too high. The excess supply of labour will then reduce wages and return the labour market to equilibrium at full employment. As wages fall firms will take on more workers and this will increase output. The interest-rate mechanism would ensure that there was always sufficient demand to purchase this output.

You can see a demonstration of the classical 'self-regulating' model by adding the following lines to Program 7.1.

```
300  W=(A-C)/(D-B)
310  NF=A+B*W
320  N=A+B*W
330  WR=W
360  U=NF-N
390  Y=G*N
590  PRINT"EMPLOYMENT (MILL)       = ";N
600  PRINT"UNEMPLOYMENT (%)        = ";U
610  PRINT"WAGE RATE               = ";WR
780  PRINT "4. SHIFT LABOUR SUPPLY"
800  IF R<1 OR R>4 THEN GOTO 790
840  IF R=4 THEN GOSUB 1200 : REM shift labour supply
1199 REM shift labour supply
1200 PRINT M$
1210 INPUT LS
1220 C=C+LS-N
1230 RETURN
```

These lines calculate the equilibrium wage (line 300) and the level of full employment (line 310). The level of employment determines output (line 390). Adding lines 780 and 840 and amending line 800 introduces a further option of shifting the labour supply (the sub-routine lines 1200 to 1230) to reflect, for example, a growing or declining labour force.

Try shifting the option variables and you will see that whilst there are effects from these changes, we always operate at full employment with a sufficiently high level of demand to purchase all the output that is produced.

The economy in this illustration is operating more effectively than any real-world economy and better than the classical economists suggested. This is because we are comparing one equilibrium position with another. In practice it would take time for markets to respond to change, and some short-term problems could arise. We can illustrate this simply by adding a further few lines to reflect an adjustment period in the labour market.

```
350  W1=W
360  U=(SN-DN)/SN
370  N=DN
380  IF DN>SN THEN N=SN
580  PRINT"FULL EMPLOYMENT (MILL) = ";NF
650  IF FF=0 THEN GOTO 700
660  GOSUB 1300 : REM continue
670  FF=0 : REM re-set flag
680  GOTO 200 : REM re-calculate
1310 PRINT"PRESS RETURN TO SEE NEXT PERIOD";
1320 INPUT Z$
1330 RETURN
```

This means unemployment may emerge, but as you will see when you run the program, it is only a temporary problem.

This model was the basis of the classical view that market economies were self-regulating. We have confined our discussion to a closed economy – that is, one where there is no foreign trade. A discussion of an open economy where expenditure on imports is a further withdrawal from the circular flow (this is part of household income that is spent but is not received by firms), and spending by people overseas on our exports is an injection, would take us beyond the scope of an introductory account. However, the classical economists believed that there was a further market mechanism which would equate imports and exports and so supply would still create its own demand. Also, we have not taken account of government's role in the circular flow. There is clearly no need for government to intervene in order to achieve full employment, but it will spend money (and that will be an injection into the circular flow) to deal with deficiencies of the market mechanism in areas such as the provision of goods and services like defence and street lighting, and some expenditure will be directed towards problems like poverty. Governments should raise the money to finance these expenditures through taxation (a withdrawal from the circular flow) and should aim for a balanced budget.

Faith in the classical view was shattered by the Great Depression of the 1930s when unemployment in the UK rose to over 20%. What was needed was a new way of looking at how market economies work, and John Maynard Keynes provided it.

7.3 The Keynesian revolution

Keynes's ideas were revolutionary – he turned the classical view upside down. For Keynes it was demand that created its own supply; mass unemployment was not caused by wages being too high, and wage cuts would not shorten the dole queues. The market economy, then, was not self-regulating. It needed to be managed by the government.

Keynes began by attacking the classical view of the interest rate mechanism. He argued that all savings would not necessarily be loaned out – some would be hoarded, that is, held as money. But why would people, or banks with whom people had deposited their savings, not take advantage of a rate of return on savings by loaning the money to firms? The problem with shares or bonds that companies issue in order to raise finance for investment is that they vary in price, so that savers could find that they make capital losses despite receiving a dividend or interest rate payment. Keynes argued that there were speculative reasons, therefore, why

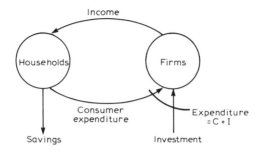

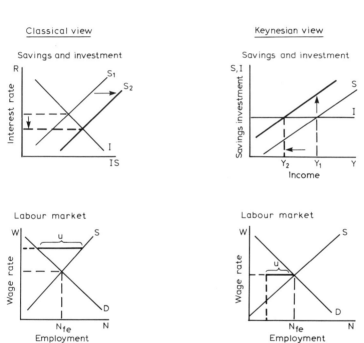

Figure 7.2 Classical and Keynesian views

people would prefer to hold their savings as money rather than incur capital losses by loaning their savings to companies. This means that the interest-rate mechanism may fail to keep savings and investment equal. For example, if an increase in saving resulting from a decision by households to spend less on consumption, is all hoarded as money, then the interest rate does not fall and there is no increase in investment. This means there is a deficiency in demand with firms unable to sell all of their output. Supply does not create its own demand.

The consequences of this are far-reaching and present a completely different view from that of the classical economists of how the market system operates. Firms unable to sell all of their output will cut back on production and lay off workers. This lowers incomes and this will reduce consumer spending – and this in turn lowers demand further. Again, firms with unsold goods will make further cutbacks and so unemployment grows. Apparently there is no halt to this downward spiral into recession. In fact the process will come to an end because lower incomes will also reduce savings so that at some point savings and investment will again be equal.

We can summarize the contrasting views between Keynes and the classicists. The latter argued that if savings and investment were not equal then interest rates would change and the overall level of demand would be maintained. For Keynes, differences between savings and investment resulted in changes in output and income, with output adjusting until it was all demanded.

You can see how the Keynesian view works through running Program 7.2.

Program 7.2 The multiplier

```
10 REM PROGRAM   MULTIPLIER
20 REM NO 7.2
50 DEF FND(V)=INT(10*V+.5)/10 : REM 1 decimal place
99 REM set initial values
100 S1=.5
110 A=-15
120 I=35
130 Y=100
140 N=0
199 REM output initial position
200 GOSUB 1000 : REM table heading
210 GOSUB 1100 : REM table year (0)
299 REM input new values
300 PRINT
310 PRINT"INPUT SAVINGS"
320 INPUT S
330 A=S-S1*Y
340 PRINT"INPUT INVESTMENT"
350 INPUT I
399 REM output results
400 PRINT
410 PRINT
420 GOSUB 1000 : REM table heading
430 FOR N=1 TO 10
440 PRINT
450 GOSUB 1100 : REM table year (N)
460 Y=Z
470 NEXT N
480 PRINT
989 REM program end
990 PRINT "END OF PROGRAM"
995 END
```

```
 998 REM subroutines
 999 REM table heading
1000 PRINT
"PERIOD";TAB(7);"OUTPUT";TAB(15);"DEMAND";TAB(23);"SAVI
NG";TAB(30);"INVESTMENT"
1010 RETURN
1099 REM fill table
1100 S=A+S1*Y
1110 C=Y-S
1120 Z=C+I
1130 PRINT
TAB(2);N;TAB(8);FND(Y);TAB(16);FND(Z);TAB(24);FND(S);TA
B(32);FND(I)
1140 RETURN

>RUN
PERIOD OUTPUT   DEMAND  SAVING INVESTMENT
    0      100      100      35      35

INPUT SAVINGS

?45
INPUT INVESTMENT
?35


PERIOD OUTPUT   DEMAND  SAVING INVESTMENT

    1      100       90      45      35

    2       90       85      40      35

    3       85     82.5    37.5      35

    4     82.5     81.3    36.3      35

    5     81.3     80.6    35.6      35

    6     80.6     80.3    35.3      35

    7     80.3     80.2    35.2      35

    8     80.2     80.1    35.1      35

    9     80.1       80      35      35

   10       80       80      35      35

END OF PROGRAM
```

You start with an initial equilibrium position and you have the option of changing either saving or investment. The table will then show you how output, demand, investment and savings vary over ten periods – for example, quarters of a year.

What you should notice is that the change in output is greater than the initial change in investment or saving. That is, the disturbance to equilibrium at the beginning is amplified by the way the market operates. This is known as the multiplier process and is examined in the next section.

Before looking at the Keynesian model more closely we ought to briefly consider the labour market mechanism. In the Keynesian view outlined above it is the lack of demand that causes unemployment, not rising wages. Imagine an economy with full employment and the equilibrium wage. An increase in savings (or a fall in investment) lowers demand and output and leads to unemployment. This unemployment will occur at the equilibrium wage-rate, and as the wage level is not 'wrong' there is no reason to see wage cuts as a means to full employment. The message is a clear one: the level of demand needs to be raised. However, the problem is that the economy has settled at an equilibrium level output which involves unemployment. If wages do fall then demand might fall further, so aggravating the problem.

These ideas brought about a revolution in policy. If the market economy was not self-regulating, it needed to be managed. If governments increased their spending or cut taxes (thus stimulating household expenditure), then this would raise demand and lower unemployment. Again, the Keynesian message was a radical one: in times of recession a budget deficit (government expenditure greater than tax revenue), not a balanced budget, was the correct approach.

7.4 The basic Keynesian model

We can now consider the Keynesian model in more detail. An equilibrium income exists when all output is bought. The value of output is income to one group or another (wages, profits, rent) and from now on we will use the terms output and income synonymously. So the condition for equilibrium is where income (Y) is equal to expenditure (E). An alternative way of expressing this, which we use in section 7.6, is where withdrawals (W) are equal to injections (J). In general withdrawals arise from savings (S), tax payments (T) and spending on imports (M) whilst injections result from investment spending (I) by firms, government expenditure (G) and exports (X) which is the spending by foreigners on a country's output.

In this section we concentrate on a basic model with households and firms but no government or foreign trade. There are two items of expenditure: consumption (C) and investment (I). Consumption is related to the level of income – higher income leads to more consumer expenditure and vice versa. We can represent this relationship by the equation

$$C = A + B.Y$$

This is a linear consumption function which is illustrated graphically by the line marked C in Figure 7.3. The first term A is known as autonomous consumption and is the amount of

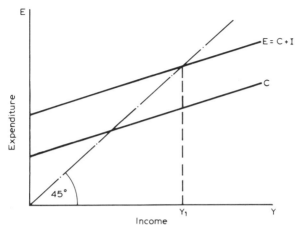

Figure 7.3 The Keynesian Income-Expenditure model

consumer spending that is not influenced by income. If the value of A changes then this shifts the consumption function upwards or downwards on the diagram. The second term B determines the amount by which consumption changes when income alters. This relationship is the marginal propensity to consume and is defined as the ratio of the change in consumption to the change in income.

Investment in the basic model is assumed to be exogenous – that is, determined outside the model. In Chapter 9 we will build a model where it will be endogenous and investment spending will be affected by changes in output. Here we will decide the level of investment spending and it will be unaffected by the level of output.

We can represent total expenditure on the diagram by adding investment to consumption expenditure. With the same scales on both axes a 45°-line represents our equilibrium condition – points where income equals expenditure. Equilibrium income is where the expenditure schedule cuts the 45° line. This provides a graphical solution for equilibrium. An alternative approach, and one that is more useful for programming purposes, is to derive a solution using some simple algebra.

$Y = E$	Equilibrium condition
$Y = C + I$	Two types of expenditure in this model.
$Y = A + B.Y + \overline{I}$	Substitute the equations for $C(= A + B.Y)$ and $I(= \overline{I})$ where the bar over the variable indicates it is exogenous

$Y - B.Y = A + \overline{I}$ by rearranging the terms

$$Y = \frac{A + \overline{I}}{1 - B}$$ This is a general solution for equilibrium income for this type of model

Program 7.3 uses this general solution and allows you to enter different values for B and I. For a given value of B you should try varying I and see after a few times whether you can predict the new level of income. Then repeat this approach with different values for B. You should remember that B is the marginal propensity to consume and whilst Keynesians assume it to be positive (i.e. increases in income lead to increases in consumer expenditure) they expect it to be less than one – that is, the change in consumption is less than the change in income because savings are also affected.

Program 7.3 Basic Keynesian model

```
 10 REM PROGRAM  BASIC KEYNESIAN MODEL
 20 REM NO 7.3
 99 REM set initial values
100 A=40
199 REM input values
200 PRINT
210 GOSUB 1000 : REM input MPC
220 GOSUB 1100 : REM input investment
299 REM calculations
300 Y=(A+I)/(1-B)
310 C=A+B*Y
499 REM output results
500 PRINT
510 PRINT"INCOME";TAB(14);Y
520 PRINT"CONSUMPTION";TAB(14);C
530 PRINT"INVESTMENT";TAB(14);I
540 PRINT"MPC";TAB(14);B
599 REM select option / input new values
600 PRINT
610 PRINT "1. TO END PROGRAM"
620 PRINT "2. TO CHANGE MPC"
630 PRINT "3. TO CHANGE INVESTMENT"
640 INPUT R
650 IF R<1 OR R>3 THEN GOTO 640
660 IF R=1 THEN GOTO 990 : REM end
670 IF R=2 THEN GOSUB 1000 : REM input MPC
680 IF R=3 THEN GOSUB 1100 : REM input investment
690 GOTO 300 : REM re-calculate
989 REM program end
990 PRINT "END OF PROGRAM"
995 END
998 REM subroutines
999 REM input MPC
1000 PRINT
1010 PRINT"INPUT VALUE OF MPC (B) ";
```

```
1020 INPUT B
1030 RETURN
1099 REM input investment
1100 PRINT
1110 PRINT"INPUT VALUE OF INVESTMENT ";
1120 INPUT I
1130 RETURN
>RUN


INPUT VALUE OF MPC (B) ?.5

INPUT VALUE OF INVESTMENT ?10

INCOME          100
CONSUMPTION     90

INVESTMENT      10
MPC             0.5

1. TO END PROGRAM
2. TO CHANGE MPC
3. TO CHANGE INVESTMENT
?1
END OF PROGRAM
```

What does the program show us? It illustrates the point made in the previous section that demand determines output – for example, a fall in investment spending will result in a lower level of national income. On the diagram the expenditure schedule would shift downwards. Furthermore the program shows the multiplier effect because changes in investment lead to larger changes in income. You should have discovered that the multiplier effect (which is measured as the ratio of the change in income to the change in investment) is greater the larger the value of the marginal propensity to consume (MPC). The significance of the MPC will be clear if we consider why the multiplier process occurs. An increase in investment raises output and incomes which in turn raises consumer expenditure. How much of the higher income is spent depends upon the MPC. This increase in consumer spending causes a further rise in demand and output which will raise incomes still further and again the MPC is crucial in deciding the subsequent change in consumption. A high value for the MPC will mean a large proportion of any change in income will be spent and this will produce a large multiplier effect, whereas a low MPC will do the reverse. The equation for the multiplier in this type of model is

$$\frac{1}{1 - MPC}$$

7.5 The basic model with government expenditure

The central policy prescription of the Keynesian revolution was the need for governments to accept the responsibility for managing the level of demand. In this section this will be done by changing government expenditure which, along with consumption and investment, is a component of aggregate demand.

If government expenditure is treated as an exogenous variable, then the equation for equilibrium income is

$$Y = \frac{A + I + G}{1 - B}$$

This is used in line 300 in Program 7.4.

Program 7.4 Inflationary and deflationary gaps

```
10 REM PROGRAM  GAP
20 REM NO 7.4
99 REM set initial values
100 I=20
110 A=40
120 FE=300
199 REM input values
200 PRINT
210 PRINT"VALUE OF MPC ";
220 INPUT B
230 PRINT
240 PRINT"GOVERNMENT EXPENDITURE ";
250 INPUT G
299 REM calculations
300  Y=(A+I+G)/(1-B)
310  Y=INT(Y+.5)
499 REM output results
500 PRINT
510 PRINT"EQUILIBRIUM INCOME ";Y
520 PRINT"FULL EMPLOY.INCOME ";FE
530 PRINT
550 IF Y=FE THEN PRINT"FULL EMPLOYMENT"
560 IF Y<FE THEN PRINT"DEFLATIONARY GAP"
570 IF Y>FE THEN PRINT"INFLATIONARY GAP"
599 REM select option
600 PRINT
610 PRINT "1. TO END PROGRAM"
620 PRINT "2. TO RE-RUN PROGRAM"
630 PRINT "3. TO INPUT NEW GOVT. EXP."
640 INPUT R
650 IF R<1 OR R>3 THEN GOTO 640
660 IF R=1 THEN GOTO 990 : REM end
670 IF R=2 THEN GOTO 100 : REM re-run
680 IF R=3 THEN GOTO 230 : REM input govt. exp.
989 REM program end
990 PRINT "END OF PROGRAM"
995 END

VALUE OF MPC ?.5

GOVERNMENT EXPENDITURE ?80

EQUILIBRIUM INCOME 280
FULL EMPLOY.INCOME 300

DEFLATIONARY GAP

1. TO END PROGRAM
2. TO RE-RUN PROGRAM
3. TO INPUT NEW GOVT. EXP.

?3
```

```
GOVERNMENT EXPENDITURE ?100

EQUILIBRIUM INCOME 320
FULL EMPLOY.INCOME 300

INFLATIONARY GAP

1. TO END PROGRAM
2. TO RE-RUN PROGRAM
3. TO INPUT NEW GOVT. EXP.
?1
END OF PROGRAM
```

This program allows you to vary government expenditure to achieve full employment. This involves deciding on a level of government spending which gives a level of aggregate demand that is just sufficient to give full employment: E 1 on Figure 7.4. If it is too low (E 2) then there is a deflationary gap indicated by the distance AB, and unemployment results. Too much spending (e.g. E 3) leads to an inflationary gap – BC on the diagram. The program allows you to select a value for MPC and the initial level

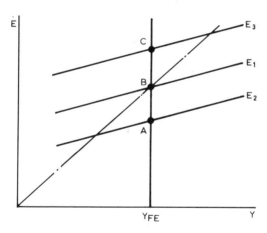

Figure 7.4 Inflationary and deflationary gaps

of government spending. Lines 550–570 checks whether full employment has been achieved and prints an appropriate message. If there is a deflationary or inflationary gap you should select option 3 and change government spending until full employment is achieved. When you are successful the option 2 will allow a rerun of the program and the selection of a different MPC. Your understanding of the multiplier should ensure that you have a better success rate than most Chancellors of the Exchequer.

7.6 The basic model and an open economy

We can now extend our basic model to include foreign trade and also introduce taxation. Recall that an alternative to the income equals expenditure condition for equilibrium is that withdrawals are equal to injections.

Injections are investment (I), government expenditure (G) and exports (X) and all three are treated as exogenous variables. In contrast the withdrawals, savings (S), taxation (T) and imports (M), are assumed to vary with income. Higher income will raise the level of savings, as we have already seen. It will also increase the tax revenue received through higher income tax payments and larger indirect tax (e.g. VAT) receipts. Higher expenditure associated with higher income levels will mean increased spending on imported goods. These relationships can be expressed in a simplified form as follows:

$$S = S1.Y$$
$$T = T1.Y$$
$$M = M1.Y$$

where the parameters $S1$, $T1$, $M1$ represent the marginal propensities to save, tax and import, respectively. The equation for equilibrium income is

$$Y = \frac{I + G + X}{S1 + T1 + M1}$$

The multiplier is

$$\frac{1}{S1 + T1 + M1}$$

that is, the multiplier effect depends upon how much of any increase in income is withdrawn from the circular flow in the form of savings, taxation and imports.

Program 7.5 Open economy model

```
 10 REM PROGRAM  OPEN
 20 REM NO 7.5
 99 REM set initial values
100 READ S1,M1,T1,I,G
110 READ X,FE
299 REM calculations
300 Y=(I+G+X)/(S1+T1+M1)
310 T=T1*Y
320 B=T-G
330 M=M1*Y
340 BP=X-M
499 REM output results
500 PRINT
520 PRINT"INCOME";TAB(20);Y
530 PRINT"F.E.  INCOME";TAB(20);FE
```

```
540 PRINT"BUDGET (-:DEFICIT)";TAB(20);B
550 PRINT"BALANCE OF PAYMENTS";TAB(20);BP
560 PRINT"GOVT. EXPEND.";TAB(20);G
570 PRINT"TAX RATE";TAB(20);T1
599 REM select option / input new values
600 PRINT
610 PRINT "1. END PROGRAM"
620 PRINT "2. INPUT NEW TAX RATE & GOVT. EXP."
630 PRINT "3. INPUT NEW GOVT. EXP."
640 INPUT R
650 IF R<1 OR R>3 THEN GOTO 640
660 IF R=1 THEN GOTO 990 : REM end
670 IF R=2 THEN GOSUB 1000 : REM input tax & govt exp
680 IF R=3 THEN GOSUB 1100 : REM input govt exp
690 GOTO 300 : REM re-calcualte
989 REM program end
990 PRINT "END OF PROGRAM"
995 END
998 REM subroutines
999 REM input tax & govt exp
1000 PRINT
1010 PRINT"INPUT NEW TAX RATE ";
1020 INPUT T1
1030 GOSUB 1100 : REM input govt exp
1040 RETURN
1099 REM input govt exp
1100 PRINT
1110 PRINT"NEW GOVT. EXPEND. ";
1120 INPUT G
1130 RETURN
2998 REM stored data
2999 REM initial values S1,M1,T1,I,G
3000 DATA .1,.2,.2,30,60
3009 REM X,FE
3010 DATA 40,300
>RUN
INCOME                  260
F.E. INCOME             300
BUDGET (-:DEFICIT)      -8
BALANCE OF PAYMENTS     -12
GOVT. EXPEND.           60
TAX RATE                0.2

1. END PROGRAM
2. INPUT NEW TAX RATE & GOVT. EXP.
3. INPUT NEW GOVT. EXP.
?3

NEW GOVT. EXPEND. ?80

INCOME                  300
F.E. INCOME             300
BUDGET (-:DEFICIT)      -20
BALANCE OF PAYMENTS     -20
GOVT. EXPEND.           80
TAX RATE                0.2
```

Program 7.5 is based on this model. It presents you with the initial position shown in the sample run and allows you to vary the tax rate and government expenditure. The budget deficit, the difference between tax revenue and government expenditure, and the balance of payments position, the difference between exports and imports are shown. Can you achieve a balanced budget (G=T) and full employment? What level of income will eliminate the balance of payments deficit?

7.7 Inflation, unemployment and balance of payments problems

Our basic Keynesian model developed in the last three sections does not include inflation or an explicit measure of unemployment. Program 7.6 will remedy this.

Program 7.6 Policy model

```
10 REM PROGRAM  POLICY
20 REM NO 7.6
99 REM set initial values
100 X=200
110 G=250
120 S1=.25
130 M1=.25
140 K=1000
200 N=1
299 REM calculations
300 Y=(G+X)/(S1+M1)
310 M=0.25*Y
320 U=2+0.02*(K-Y)
330 P=24-2*U
499 REM output results
500 PRINT
510 PRINT"YEAR ";N
520 PRINT
530 PRINT"CAPACITY";TAB(16);K
540 PRINT"OUTPUT";TAB(16);Y
550 PRINT"GOVT. EXPEND.";TAB(16);G
560 PRINT"EXPORTS";TAB(16);X
570 PRINT"IMPORTS";TAB(16);M
580 PRINT"UNEMPLOYMENT";TAB(16);U
590 PRINT"INFLATION";TAB(16);P
600 PRINT
610 IF N=8 THEN GOTO 990 : REM end
619 REM calculate new capacity/exports
620 X=X+75-6.25*P
630 K=K+100
640 PRINT"YEAR ";N+1
650 PRINT"CAPACITY ";K
660 PRINT"EXPORTS  ";X
669 REM input govt exp
670 PRINT
680 PRINT"INPUT GOVT. EXPEN. (-1 TO END)";
690 INPUT G
700 IF G=-1 THEN GOTO 990 : REM end
749 REM next year
750 N=N+1
760 IF N<9 THEN GOTO 300 : REM re-calculate
989 REM  program end
990 PRINT "END OF PROGRAM"
995 END

>RUN

YEAR 1

CAPACITY        1000
OUTPUT          900
GOVT. EXPEND.   250
EXPORTS         200
IMPORTS         225
UNEMPLOYMENT    4
INFLATION       16
```

```
YEAR 2
CAPACITY 1100
EXPORTS   175

INPUT GOVT. EXPEN. (-1 TO END)?225

YEAR 2
CAPACITY        1100
OUTPUT          800
GOVT. EXPEND.   225
EXPORTS         175
IMPORTS         200
UNEMPLOYMENT    8
INFLATION       8
```

The basic model is a simplified version of Program 7.5 with taxation and investment excluded. You can manipulate government spending to alter output in an attempt to achieve low unemployment, low inflation and a surplus on the balance of payments by year 5 or 6.

Unemployment depends upon how close output is to capacity (line 320). Capacity represents the output that gives full employment which in this program is 2%. Capacity grows by 100 each year, reflecting the growth of the economy arising from factors like technological change.

Unemployment affects inflation (line 330) through what is known as the Phillips curve. Lower unemployment is associated with higher inflation. This relationship is the subject of some dispute and is considered more fully in the next chapter. However, in this program, an increase in aggregate demand which reduces unemployment causes an increase in inflationary pressures.

The inflation rate affects the competitiveness of exports (line 620). If inflation falls below the world rate, here assumed to be 12%, then exports rise and vice versa. Together with imports which are affected by the level of output (line 310), this determines the balance of payments position.

The position of the economy you inherit in year 1 is shown in the sample run. You have to make a decision about government expenditure in year 2. You will see that the capacity is not under your influence and the level of exports is determined by the inflation rate of the previous year.

In trying to secure the surplus on the balance of payments by year 5 or 6 you will discover some of the problems that have confronted post-war Chancellors of the Exchequer. Try to produce full employment by year 8, the year of the general election. You get three or four years longer than most Chancellors because you are a beginner. On the other hand you can always find out how this fictional economy works by looking at the program listing, which no occupant of No. 11 can do with the real economy.

EXERCISES

(7.1) Modify Program 7.4 to calculate the size of the deflationary or inflationary gap. Figure 7.4 should help you in this task. You will see from the diagram that you need to calculate the level of aggregate demand at the full employment level of income.

(7.2) In Program 7.5 Government expenditure is exogenous, which is a normal assumption of simple models. However, lower levels of income imply higher unemployment, which tends to raise government spending on unemployment and supplementary benefits. The reverse tends to happen when income levels rise. Modify the program so that total government (TG) spending is equal to the level you input (G) and an amount which varies with income (G1.Y) i.e. TG = G − G1 * Y. You will have to assign a value to G1. Also you need to modify the equilibrium condition in line 300 – this requires some simple algebra, but remember that in equilibrium withdrawals equal injections.

(7.3) Program 7.6 can be modified and extended in many ways. Below are a number of suggestions and exercises.

(i)   Modify the program to include an opinion poll where your rating depends on your success in keeping unemployment and inflation low and avoiding a balance of payments deficit.

(ii)   Modify the program to include investment. The results of this are not very interesting so introduce the following modification. Let investment be related to the level of income on the grounds that higher output will encourage firms to spend more on capital equipment. (Chapter 9 will introduce you to a different and more conventional link between output and investment.) Then let capacity of the economy be affected by the amount of investment. Other things being equal, a larger capital stock will tend to increase the capacity output of the economy.

(iii) Modify the program to allow an option to introduce an incomes policy. The experience has often been that whilst an incomes policy lowers inflation in the short run, this is followed by a wages and prices explosion at a later date. You could incorporate this in your program.

(iv)   A devaluation option could be introduced. Devaluation improves a country's competitivenes, so other things being equal, imports tend to be less and exports more. Confine the effects to exports. Devaluation also tends to raise a country's inflation rate so you should include this effect.

Chapter 8

Monetarism

8.1 The rise of monetarism

The Keynesian approach to economic policy, described in the last chapter, was adopted as the basis for managing the economy in the UK for more than 30 years after the Second World War. However, during the 1970s this approach was increasingly challenged. One reason for doubting the correctness of the Keynesian policy was the poor performance of the economy which experienced both higher unemployment and inflation rates. The latter caused particular concern with double-digit inflation rates for half the 1970s and an annual rate of 25% in 1975. At the same time there was an intellectual challenge to Keynesian ideas from monetarism. Monetarism was appealing to many people because it seemed to address itself to what had become a central economic problem: inflation. It suggested that government could control inflation by an appropriate money supply policy. But monetarism is more than an anti-inflation policy. It attacks the foundations of Keynesian thinking by arguing that markets are self-regulating and therefore demand management policies are unnecessary. Furthermore, Keynesian reflation policies designed to reduce unemployment will either be totally ineffective, or only have a temporary impact at a cost of higher inflation.

In this chapter we will explain the background to this 'monetarist counter-revolution' by examining the importance of money and the attack on Keynesian demand management policies. We will see why Mrs Thatcher's governments not only rejected calls to boost public spending but have embarked upon a policy of expenditure cuts in a period which experienced the highest unemployment rates since the 1930s.

8.2 The quantity theory of money

Monetarists believe that the rate of increase in the money supply determines the rate of inflation. They subscribe to the quantity theory of money. We can best understand their position (and that of those who oppose it) by considering first of all a relationship that is indisputable.

The amount of money spent in an economy, in a given period, will be equal to the stock of money (M), which comprises cash (notes and coins) and bank deposits (because people can also pay for goods and services by cheque) multiplied by the number of times it is used, or its velocity or circulation (V). This amount must be equal to the value of goods bought, which in turn is equal to a measure of goods and services produced (O) multiplied by an index of prices (P) at which they are sold.

$$M.V \equiv P.O$$

This is an identity – something which is true by definition. We can underline this point if we consider how the velocity of circulation is measured. As we cannot keep track of every pound note that is spent, the only way we can know the value of the velocity of circulation is dividing the money value of goods bought by money supply:

$$V \equiv \frac{P.O}{M}$$

alternatively

$$V \equiv \frac{Y}{M}$$

where Y is the nominal or (money) value of national income.

The monetarists turn this indisputable relationship into a controversial theory by making certain hypotheses about the behaviour of variables. First, they argue that the money supply is an exogenous variable that can be controlled by the government. Secondly, the velocity of circulation is regarded as stable. Combining these two propositions means that if the government expands the money supply then monetary spending increases so either prices or output must increase. The final monetarist hypothesis is that market forces operate to move the economy to full employment (see section 8.3). This means that increases in the money supply raise prices

$$\overset{\uparrow}{M} \; \overset{\longrightarrow}{\overline{V}} = \overset{\uparrow}{P} \; \overline{O}$$

This gives the monetarist explanation of inflation

$$\Delta M \rightarrow \Delta P$$

The policy prescription is clear: reducing the rate of monetary growth will lower the inflation rate. Of course the effect is not instantaneous, and monetarists like Milton Friedman have suggested that inflation may take one or even two years to respond to money supply changes. Furthermore, as we will see later, output may be affected in the short run, but monetarists believe that ultimately increases in the money supply result in rising prices.

This view of money is not shared by all economists. Indeed it is only in the last decade that serious consideration has been given to controlling the money supply, and only since 1979 has it been a prominent feature of government policy. Early post-war Keynesians did not believe that the velocity of circulation was stable. A tight monetary policy would restrict the growth of the money supply compared with the amount demanded and this would lead to some rise in interest rates which, in turn, would persuade people to demand and hold less money. In other words, the velocity of circulation would rise.

In terms of the quantity theory, the extreme version of this view would be represented by

$$\overset{\downarrow \rightarrow \uparrow}{M.V} = P.O \qquad \text{i.e. } \Delta M \rightarrow \Delta V.$$

This view stresses the wide range of financial assets that are 'money substitutes'. This is linked to a point many Keynesians would wish to emphasize: the problem of defining 'money'. There is no dispute that cash and current account bank deposits (sight deposits) should be counted as money and this is the M1 measure used in the UK. The definition could be broader to include deposit accounts (time deposits), and essentially this is the M3 measure of money. But why not extend the definition to include deposits with building societies or other highly liquid financial assets? Wherever the line is drawn, there will always be some financial assets which we can call 'near money'. It is these financial assets which Keynesians argue can act as money substitutes. Defining 'money' is of practical importance. If governments are to regulate money supply, they need to know which measure to control.

Over the last 25 years there has been growing acceptance by Keynesians that changes in the money supply *do* influence the level of spending. However, they do not necessarily accept that it is the dominant influence that monetarists suggest, although some Keynesians, particularly in the UK, have not abandoned their views about the variability of V. Criticism of the quantity theory in recent years has been concentrated on the effect of changes in the money supply on the right-hand side of the equation. These critics challenge the monetarist view that market economies tend towards full employment. If there are unemployed resources then an expansionary monetary policy could raise output and employment. Similarly a tight monetary policy would reduce spending and this would lower output and raise unemployment. In its extreme form this view suggests that

$$\Delta M \rightarrow \Delta O$$

But would not prices and inflation be affected? This depends on how far unemployment levels influence wage increases which in turn determine how much prices are raised. This view can be represented as follows:

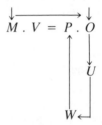

Cost-push
pressure

The relationship between unemployment and wage or price inflation is known as the 'Phillips curve', a concept that we encountered in Chapter 7. Keynesians generally take the view that, over a fairly wide range of unemployment rates, the level of demand (and unemployment is an indicator of this) has little effect on the rate of wage and price inflation. Under these circumstances other influences are important. Cost-push pressure, arising from attempts to maintain or improve real wages, or action by some groups of workers to improve their position in the wage league table which, if resisted by other workers, will push up wages generally, may be important sources of rising inflation. That is, there may be price-wage and wage-wage spirals operating. These will tend to push the Phillips curve upwards. A further influence which may move the curve in the opposite direction is an incomes policy.

Demand pressures may exert a more powerful influence on inflation if the economy is operating at near-full capacity. In which case unemployment will be very low and excess demand in some markets for goods and services, and sections of the làbour market, will lead to rising prices. However, Keynesians would not regard this type of 'demand-pull' inflation as an explanation of the UK's inflation rates in the last 15 years, since the economy has been operating with spare capacity for most of the period. However, demand may have a more important influence on inflation if unemployment levels are pushed high enough to weaken the cost-push pressures and exert a downward influence on the rate of wage and price inflation.

The Keynesian opposition to the monetarist anti-inflation policy is clear: there are likely to be very heavy unemployment costs to bringing inflation down.

Program 8.1 aims to demonstrate these differences between Keynesians and monetarists. Option 1 shows the simple monetarist view with a stable velocity of circulation and output always at the full-employment level, which here corresponds to 5% unemployment rate. Option 2 builds in a time-lag between changes in the money supply and inflation, so in the short run velocity will not appear stable. For example, a more rapid rate of increase in the money supply will not cause higher inflation immediately, so the measured velocity of circulation will fall. However, if this rate of monetary expansion is maintained then the velocity becomes stable again. In the Keynesian option the effect on output and unemployment can be seen. If monetary expansion is less than inflation, this exerts a contractionary influence on the economy and output falls which raises unemployment. Higher unemployment, via a Phillips curve, lowers inflation but this effect is small unless unemployment rises above 10%. When unemployment levels are very low, below 3%, monetary expansion starts to have a greater effect in raising inflation.

Program 8.1 Quantity theory of money

```
10 REM PROGRAM  QUANTITY THEORY
20 REM NO 8.1
50 DEF FND(X)=INT(100*X+.5)/100 : REM2 decimal places
99 REM set initial values
100 READ ML,V,PL,O
110 READ M,P,Y,U
120 P1=10
130 ML1=ML*(1+.01*M)
199 REM select option
200 PRINT "CHOOSE OPTION"
210 PRINT
220 PRINT"1. SIMPLE MONETARIST VIEW"
230 PRINT"2. MONETARIST VIEW WITH TIME LAG"
240 PRINT"3. KEYNESIAN VIEW"
250 INPUT R
260 IF R<1 OR R>3 THEN GOTO 250
490 PRINT
499 REM output results
```

```
500 PRINT"MONEY X VELOCITY = PRICE LEVEL X OUTPUT"
510 PRINT"  M   .    V   =    P    .    O"
520 PRINT
530 PRINT
TAB(1);FND(ML);TAB(12);FND(V);TAB(23);FND(PL);TAB(34);FND(O)

540 PRINT
550 PRINT"NOMINAL INCOME";TAB(22);FND(Y)
560 PRINT"MONEY SUPPLY GROWTH";TAB(22);FND(M)
570 PRINT"INFLATION";TAB(22);FND(P)
580 PRINT"UNEMPLOYMENT RATE";TAB(22);FND(U)
590 PRINT
599 REM input values & calculations
600 PRINT"INPUT MONEY SUPPLY CHANGE (%)"
610 PRINT"(-1 TO END PROGRAM)   ";
620 INPUT M
630 IF M=-1 THEN GOTO 990 : REM end
639 REM calculate
640 ML=ML*(1+.01*M)
650 PL1=PL
660 IF R=1 THEN GOSUB 1000 : REM simple monetarist
670 IF R=2 THEN GOSUB 1100 : REM monetarist & time lag
680 IF R=3 THEN GOSUB 1200 : REM keynesian
690 P=((PL-PL1)/PL1)*100
700 Y=FL*O
750 GOTO 490 : REM output results
989 REM program end
990 PRINT "END OF PROGRAM"
995 END
998 REM subroutines
999 REM simple monetarist
1000 PL=(ML*V)/O
1010 RETURN
1099 REM monetarist & time lag
1100 V=5
1110 PL=(ML1*V)/O
1120 V=(PL*O)/ML
1130 ML1=ML1*(1+.01*M)
1140 RETURN
1199 REM keynesian
1200 O=100
1210 O1=(ML*V)/(PL1*(1+.01*P1))
1220 U=5+.75*(O-O1)
1230 IF U<1 THEN U=1
1240 PL=PL*(1+.01*P1)
1250 K=1
1260 IF U<3 OR U>10 THEN K=2
1270 P1=15-(K*U)
1280 IF P1<2 THEN P1=2
1290 O=O1
1300 RETURN
2998 REM stored data
2999 REM initial values ML,V,PL,O
3000 DATA 20,5,1,100
3009 REM M,P,Y,U
3010 DATA 10,10,100,5
>RUN
CHOOSE OPTION


1. SIMPLE MONETARIST VIEW
2. MONETARIST VIEW WITH TIME LAG
3. KEYNESIAN VIEW
?1


MONEY X VELOCITY = PRICE LEVEL X OUTPUT
  M   .    V   =    P    .    O

 20        5        1        100
```

```
NOMINAL INCOME          100
MONEY SUPPLY GROWTH     10
INFLATION               10
UNEMPLOYMENT RATE        5

INPUT MONEY SUPPLY CHANGE (%)
(-1 TO END PROGRAM)   ?5

MONEY X VELOCITY = PRICE LEVEL X OUTPUT
   M   .     V    =      P      .    O


  21         5          1.05         100

NOMINAL INCOME          105
MONEY SUPPLY GROWTH      5
INFLATION                5
UNEMPLOYMENT RATE        5

INPUT MONEY SUPPLY CHANGE (%)
(-1 TO END PROGRAM)   ?-1

END OF PROGRAM
```

At this stage the Keynesian version may appear a better explanation, because it will allow unemployment to vary. This outcome and the critical view of monetarism arises from the Keynesian view of the Phillips curve. Before reaching any conclusions on this debate, we need to consider the monetarist version of the Phillips curve.

8.3 Monetarist view of the Phillips curve

The monetarist analysis of the labour market lies at the centre of their view that market economies are self-regulating, and their explanation of the Phillips curve.

The labour market, according to monetarists, tends towards equilibrium and is therefore essentially the same as in the classical view outlined in the previous chapter. However, we now need to take a closer look at this market. In Figure 8.1 you will see that demand for and supply of labour are related to the real wage (W/P), that is, the money wage deflated by the price level. Firms in determining their demand for labour are interested in the money wage they pay workers in relation to the price they can get for their product. What causes them to demand fewer workers is when money wages rise faster than prices. Similarly workers, when they supply their services, are interested in the money wage in relation to the price they pay for the products they buy.

Monetarists believe that market forces ensure that the labour markets tend to clear i.e. move to the equilibrium. This requires money wages and prices to be sufficiently flexible to restore the equilibrium real wage following any disturbance. The unemployment associated with equilibrium is called the natural rate of unemployment. We will consider this concept in more detail in the next section.

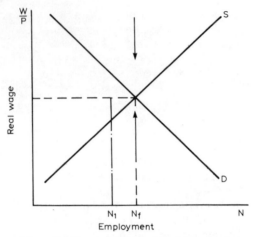

Figure 8.1 Monetarist view of the labour market

Changes in real wages occur when there is excess demand or supply. We cannot directly observe excess demand, but an indicator of it will be the unemployment rate, so

$$\Delta(W/P) = f(U)$$

that is, the change in real wages is a function of unemployment. As the change in real wages is the difference between the change in money wages and inflation, this relationship can be represented as follows

$$\Delta W - \Delta P = f(U)$$

or alternatively

$$\Delta W = f(U) + \Delta P$$

that is, the increase in money wages is related to unemployment plus the rate of inflation. The inflation rate that is relevant to determining the increase in wages is the expected inflation rate. So the monetarist view of the Phillips curve can be written as

$$\Delta W = f(U) + \Delta PE$$

This seemingly minor and reasonable modification to the Phillips curve has profound implications, as we will see.

Program 8.2 allows you to explore the inflation-unemployment relationship of this monetarist view. In the program and the explanation below, two simplifying assumptions are made. First, we shall assume that the rate of price inflation is equal to wage inflation. More realistically, wage increases can be partly offset by productivity improvements so prices would not normally rise as fast as wages, but our assumption makes events easier to follow and does not produce essentially different conclusions. Secondly, we need to decide how expectations of inflation are determined. We follow the 'adaptive expectations' approach, i.e. assume that expectations are adapted in the light of past experience. In our case, we assume that the expected inflation rate this year is equal to the actual rate last year. More sophisticated approaches have been developed (for example, people may have longer memories than we seem to assume!) but again, the simple approach does produce the same type of results as the more complicated models.

Program 8.2 Expectations augmented Phillips curve

```
  10 REM PROGRAM  EXPECT
  20 REM NO 8.2
  99 REM set initial values
 100 PE=0
 199 REM input value
 200 PRINT
 210 PRINT"INPUT UNEMPLOYMENT RATE"
 215 PRINT"(-1 TO END PROGRAM) ";
 220 INPUT U
 230 IF U=-1 THEN GOTO 990 : REM end
 299 REM calculations
 300 P=10-2*U +PE
 499 REM output results
 500 PRINT
 510 PRINT"INFLATION RATE";TAB(25);P
 520 PRINT"EXPECTED INFLATION RATE";TAB(25);PE
 530 PRINT"UNEMPLOYMENT RATE";TAB(25);U
 540 PRINT
 550 PE=P
 560 GOTO 210 : REM input new value
 989 REM program end
 990 PRINT "END OF PROGRAM"
 995 END
>RUN

INPUT UNEMPLOYMENT RATE
(-1 TO END PROGRAM) ?3

INFLATION RATE           4
EXPECTED INFLATION RATE  0
UNEMPLOYMENT RATE        3

INPUT UNEMPLOYMENT RATE
(-1 TO END PROGRAM) ?3

INFLATION RATE           8
EXPECTED INFLATION RATE  4
UNEMPLOYMENT RATE        3
```

If we start with zero inflation and no expected inflation with an unemployment rate of 5% (the same as the position you inherit in the program), then expansionary government policies which reduce unemployment to 3% result in inflation of 4% (see Figure 8.2) i.e. we move up the Phillips curve from A to B.

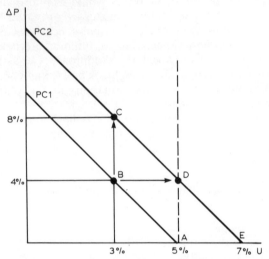

Figure 8.2 Monetarist view of the Phillips curve

But people will adapt to the new rate of inflation and the expected rate will rise from zero to 4%. In terms of the diagram, the Phillips curve shifts upwards to PC2. Recall that inflation is related to both unemployment and expected inflation, so as Figure 8.2 only shows the relationship between inflation and unemployment, we have a different Phillips curve for every expected inflation rate.

This presents the government with a dilemma. If unemployment is to be kept at 3% then inflation will rise to 8% (B to C on figure 8.2); on the other hand, if the government does not expand demand further and inflation remains at 4%, unemployment will rise and return to the 5% rate (B to D). Furthermore, as Figure 8.2 shows, an unemployment rate of 7% will be needed to reduce inflation back to zero (D to E). You should explore the relationships involved in this model by running the program.

You should discover that the 5% unemployment rate is rather special. It is the only one that gives a stable inflation rate and a position where actual and expected inflation rates are equal. It is the natural rate of unemployment (UN) referred to earlier. If unemployment is less than UN, the inflation rate rises and the actual rate of inflation is greater than that expected. When unemployment is above UN, the opposite conditions hold.

There are some very important implications for government policy in this analysis. Reducing inflation requires unemployment above the natural rate, and the more unemployment we are prepared to tolerate, the more rapidly inflation can be brought down. It is because the elimination of high inflation rates would require high unemployment that monetarists like Milton Friedman advocate a gradualist approach, with governments setting targets to reduce inflation over a four- or five-year period. When inflation has been reduced to an acceptable level, the economy will return to the natural rate of unemployment.

The monetarist view of the Phillips curve leads to a major attack on Keynesian demand management policy, and this is explored in the next section.

8.4 The monetarist attack on Keynesian policy activism

Keynesians, as we saw in the previous chapter, advocate expanding demand as a means of reducing unemployment. Monetarists argue that this is not an option open to governments except in the short term and at the cost of accelerating inflation.

The analysis of the previous section can be represented as follows:

$$U = UN + f(\Delta PE - \Delta P)$$
$$\underset{\text{Lag}}{\uparrow\underline{\hspace{2cm}}}$$

Unemployment can only be pushed below the natural rate if inflation is greater than the expected rate. But given adaptive expectations the actual rate will come to be expected – in our illustration, after one year. So, according to the monetarists, we could expand demand through raising the rate of monetary growth, which will produce an inflation greater than that expected, but the effect is only short-lived unless we are prepared to raise monetary growth and inflation at an accelerating rate.

To understand this point more fully, we need to recall the monetarist view that the labour market tends to clear – market forces move the economy to the equilibrium real wage and the natural rate of unemployment. This real wage is consistent with a variety of inflation rates – a particular real wage only requires money wages and prices to rise at the same rate. So when expected and actual rates of inflation rates are equal, the economy moves to the natural unemployment rate. Indeed the economy would not move from that point even if the inflation rate were to change providing expectations adjusted immediately. But expectations are, here, considered to be adaptive so changes in inflation will not be correctly anticipated straight away and for this reason unemployment rates different from the natural rate may occur, as the equation above shows. As Friedman says, 'only surprises matter', and we cannot surprise people without experiencing what governments, and their electorates, would regard as unacceptable, namely accelerating inflation. At some point we will have to step off the escalator.

You can explore this view more thoroughly with Program 8.3. In it, the rate of monetary growth leads to the same rate of inflation a year later.

Program 8.3 Adaptive expectations

```
 10 REM PROGRAM
 20 REM NO 8.3
 99 REM set initial values
100 UN=5
110 A=.5
120 M=0
130 P=0
200 FOR N=1 TO 8
299 REM calculations
300 PE=P
310 P=M
320 U=UN+A*(PE-P)
499 REM output results
500 PRINT
510 PRINT"YEAR ";N
520 PRINT
530 PRINT"UNEMPLOYMENT RATE";TAB(25);U
540 PRINT"INFLATION RATE";TAB(25);P
580 IF N=8 THEN GOTO 700
599 REM input value
600 PRINT "MONEY SUPPLY CHANGE";TAB(21);
610 INPUT M
700 NEXT N
710 PRINT
989 REM program end
990 PRINT "END OF PROGRAM"
995 END
>RUN

YEAR 1

UNEMPLOYMENT RATE        5
INFLATION RATE           0
MONEY SUPPLY CHANGE   ?4

YEAR 2

UNEMPLOYMENT RATE        3
INFLATION RATE           4
MONEY SUPPLY CHANGE   ?4

YEAR 3

UNEMPLOYMENT RATE        5
INFLATION RATE           4
MONEY SUPPLY CHANGE   ?
```

The monetarist explanation so far has assumed that expectations are formed adaptively. But as Program 8.3 illustrates, this essentially 'backward-looking' way of deciding the expected inflation rate can lead to people persistently underpredicting inflation when inflation rates are rising and vice versa. Some monetarists argue that this implies irrational behaviour. They suggest that if expectations were formed 'rationally', use would be made of information available at the time. This would include information on policy changes made by the government.

An illustration will make the significance of the 'rational expectations' view clearer. If it is believed that changes in the money supply cause inflation, people will take account of monetary growth when forming expectations of inflation. If there were perfect knowledge of these changes and their effects then the expected and actual inflation rates would be equal and the unemployment rate would equal the natural rate. In these circumstances policy activism (macro policy designed to influence output and unemployment) would be impotent and the short-run Phillips curve would be vertical. Of course, knowledge is not perfect. So this approach, often called the 'new classical' view, can be expressed as:

$$U = UN + e$$

where e represents an errors term arising from the difference between actual and expected inflation. But this does not really lessen the attack on Keynesian demand management policy because the errors must be random, without any systematic pattern to them. If this were not so, then this would provide information which would be incorporated into a rationally formed expectation. Any systematic government policy would then be anticipated.

This is a radically different conclusion to that of the Keynesians, and it is not surprising that governments who share the monetarist view resist calls to reflate the economy in order to lower unemployment, and argue that the role of macro policy is the elimination of inflation, not the reduction of the dole queues.

8.5 How can unemployment be reduced?

If Keynesian demand management policies cannot be used to reduce unemployment, either because they are ineffective or have only a temporary effect at the cost of higher inflation, can anything be done? Whilst monetarists argue that unemployment should not be pushed below the natural rate, they do suggest a number of policies which could be used to reduce the natural rate itself.

Recall that the natural rate is the unemployment rate associated with equilibrium in the labour market. This arises partly because of frictions in the market due to lack of information and immobility. Policies designed to reduce these frictions, for example, changes in the housing market to increase geographical mobility, would lower the natural rate. Unemployment may be voluntary if the difference between wages in work and the state benefits received by the unemployed are insufficient to provide an incentive to seek a job. Some monetarists suggest that lower real benefit payments would lower the natural rate.

This controversial option is incorporated in Program 8.4, which in other respects is the same as Program 8.3.

Program 8.4 Natural rate of unemployment

```
 10 REM PROGRAM
 20 REM NO 8.4
 99 REM set initial values
100 UN=5
110 A=.5
120 M=0
130 P=0
140 B=0
200 FOR N=1 TO 8
299 REM calculations
300 PE=P
310 P=M
320 UN=UN+.1*B
330 U=UN+A*(PE-P)
499 REM output results
500 PRINT
510 PRINT "YEAR ";N
520 PRINT
530 PRINT"UNEMPLOYMENT RATE";TAB(25);U
540 PRINT"INFLATION RATE";TAB(25);P
580 IF N=8 THEN GOTO 700
599 REM input new values
600 PRINT"MONEY SUPPLY CHANGE";TAB(21);
610 INPUT M
620 PRINT"CHANGE IN BENEFITS(%)";
630 INPUT B
700 NEXT N
750 PRINT
989 REM program end
990 PRINT "END OF PROGRAM"
995 END
>RUN

YEAR 1

UNEMPLOYMENT RATE        5
INFLATION RATE           0
MONEY SUPPLY CHANGE   ?0
CHANGE IN BENEFITS(%)?-10

YEAR 2

UNEMPLOYMENT RATE        4
INFLATION RATE           0
MONEY SUPPLY CHANGE   ?0
CHANGE IN BENEFITS(%)?0

YEAR 3

UNEMPLOYMENT RATE        4
INFLATION RATE           0
MONEY SUPPLY CHANGE   ?
```

8.6 How can the money supply be reduced?

In this chapter we have seen why monetarists regard Keynesian macro policies as being ineffective in reducing unemployment, so they would reject calls for a reflationary policy of tax cuts and government expenditure increases. If governments want to assist market forces to increase employment, they should pursue micro policies, of the type indicated in the last section, designed to improve the workings of the labour market. Macro policy should be directed at reducing the rate of inflation through a control of the money supply. Governments have a special responsibility in this matter. Most monetarists believe the rate of monetary expansion is ultimately determined by the actions of the government.

Government spending has to be financed. Tax revenue is clearly a major source of finance, but for most of the post-war period insufficient money has been raised in this way so the government has been running a budget deficit which has given rise to a borrowing requirement.

Essentially there are two ways the Public Sector Borrowing Requirement (PSBR) can be financed: through increasing the money supply or by borrowing from the public. If all of the budget deficit were covered by borrowing from the public (through selling long-term debt-bonds or gilt-edged securities) there need be no increase in the money supply as government spending, which puts money into the economy, is exactly matched by a money flow from the private sector arising from tax payments and lending to the government. However, people will only lend to the government if

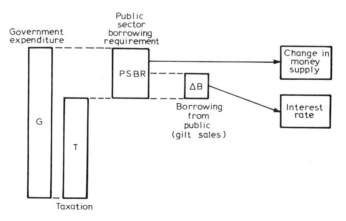

Figure 8.3 The PSBR and control of the money supply

it offers to pay a high-enough interest rate to make it an attractive proposition. The basic framework is shown in Figure 8.3.

We can now see one of the major reasons why Mrs Thatcher's government has tried to cut government expenditure at a time of record unemployment levels. Monetary targets have been announced with a view to reducing inflation, and to prevent very high interest rates being produced by heavy borrowing (B), PSBR limits have been set. The government wishes to cut taxes (T) to increase incentives, so-called 'supply-side' policies, which it is claimed will increase opportunities and willingness to work. The PSBR limits therefore require cuts in government spending (G).

In this and the previous chapter we have outlined the Keynesian and monetarist positions. It is a debate over important issues: how market economies behave and the role of government. In the next chapter we consider some extensions to these basic macro models.

EXERCISES

(8.1) The velocity of circulation is likely to be affected by interest rates since, other things being equal, lower interest rates are likely to encourage people to hold more money, thus lowering the velocity. The interest rate is likely to be affected by the rate of monetary growth in the short run, with an expansionary monetary policy lowering interest rates. Write a program to capture these effects. An expansionary monetary policy is one where the rate of monetary growth is greater than the rate of inflation in the previous period. Compare the effects with those in Program 8.2.

(8.2) Using program 8.3:

(a) Devise monetary policy to achieve the following unemployment rates

Year:	1	2	3	4	5	6	7	8	9
Unemployment:	5	5	3	3	3	4	4	5	5

(b) devise a monetary policy to reduce inflation to zero by year 16, creating as small an increase in unemployment as possible.

(c) compare the results you obtain in (b) with those you would get if you reduced inflation to zero in year 12.

(8.3) The following data relates to the UK for the period 1972–83.

Table 8.1

Year	Change in money supply (% p.a.)	Inflation rate (%)	Unemployment rate (%)
1972	26.8	7.3	3.7
1973	26.4	9.1	2.6
1974	10.3	15.8	2.6
1975	6.6	24.3	3.9
1976	9.7	16.6	5.2
1977	9.6	15.8	5.6
1978	12.3	8.3	5.5
1979	13.2	13.5	5.1
1980	18.7	17.9	6.4
1981	24.7	11.9	9.9
1982	9.3	8.6	11.5
1983	10.6	4.6	12.3

Plot on a graph inflation and the change in the money supply for the whole period. On a separate graph with inflation on the vertical axis and unemployment on the horizontal, plot the observations for the period 1972 to 1983.

Compare the pattern you get from the UK data with the one you obtained from exercise 8.2.

(8.4) Extend Program 8.3 to allow the relationship between the PSBR, interest rates and the money supply as outlined in section 8.5 to be incorporated.

Chapter 9

Extensions to the macro model

9.1 Introduction

Our introduction to macro economics in the previous two chapters
has involved considering basic Keynesian and monetarist models.
In this chapter we will construct a model that uses elements of both
approaches by combining the Keynesian interest in total
expenditure with a money market which allows the money supply
to have an influence. But we begin by considering some simple
dynamic macro models.

9.2 Dynamic models – the lagged multiplier

Dynamic models involve the explicit consideration of time. Most
of the models in Chapter 7 were 'comparative static', that is, they
could be used to compare one equilibrium level with another, but
could not indicate how long it would take to move from one
equilibrium to another, nor show what path would be followed. As
with the cobweb theorem, discussed in Chapter 3, we will find that
when time is introduced into macro models, fluctuations may
occur and sometimes new equilibrium positions are never reached.

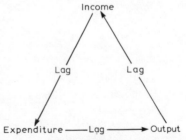

Figure 9.1 Time lags and the circular flow

Recall the circular flow of income, introduced in Chapter 7,
where the value of output produced by firms was received as
income by households who in turn spent part of it. There are likely

116

to be time-lags in the circular flow of income as illustrated in Figure 9.1. We shall ignore the lag between output and income but we shall consider an example of each of the other two.

Suppose consumer expenditure is related to the previous period's income, that is, it takes time to adjust expenditure to new income levels. This could be represented as:

$$C_t = A + B.Y_{t-1}$$

This is the type of consumption function used in Program 9.1. You select the value of the marginal propensity to consume (i.e. the value of B in the equation above) and a new level of investment. The program then calculates income levels for the next 10 periods, and shows how the multiplier works through time. This gives a fairly smooth convergence towards the new equilibrium. If the time lag in this case was a quarter, then most of the multiplier effect is felt in the first year.

Program 9.1 The dynamic multiplier

```
 10 REM PROGRAM  MULTIPLIER
 20 REM NO  9.1
 50 DEF FND(V)=INT(10*V+0.5)/10 : REM one decimal place
 99 REM set initial values
100 A=20
110 I=30
199 REM input values & calculate
200 PRINT
210 PRINT "INPUT M.P.C. ";
220 INPUT B
230 PRINT
240 Y=(A+I)/(1-B)
250 PRINT "EQUILIBRIUM INCOME ";FND(Y)
260 PRINT "INVESTMENT = ";I
270 PRINT "Input new investment ";
280 INPUT I
499 REM output results & calculate
500 PRINT
510 PRINT TAB(1);"PERIOD";TAB(13);"INCOME";TAB(25);"CONSUMPTION"
520 PRINT
530 FOR T=1 TO 10
540 Y1=Y
550 C=A+B*Y1
560 Y=C+I
570 PRINT TAB(1);T;TAB(15);FND(Y);TAB(28);FND(C)
580 NEXT T
599 REM re-run option
600 PRINT
610 PRINT "1. To END program"
620 PRINT "2. To RUN it again"
630 INPUT R
640 IF R<1 OR R>2 THEN GOTO 630
650 IF R=2 THEN GOTO 100 : REM re-run
989 REM program end
990 PRINT"END OF PROGRAM"
995 END
```

```
    >

INPUT M.P.C. ?.5

EQUILIBRIUM INCOME 100
INVESTMENT = 30
Input new investment ?40

    PERIOD       INCOME       CONSUMPTION

    1            110          70
    2            115          75
    3            117.5        77.5
    4            118.8        78.8
    5            119.4        79.4
    6            119.7        79.7
    7            119.8        79.8
    8            119.9        79.9
    9            120          80
    10           120          80

1. To END program
2. To RUN it again
?1
END OF PROGRAM
```

This model is now extended to incorporate a lag between expenditure and output.

9.3 An inventory model

Firms cannot adjust output immediately to meet a change in demand though, in practice, they try to anticipate these changes. In the model used in Program 9.3 there is a one-period lag between demand (consumption plus investment) and output. However, firms carry stocks or inventories of goods to help cope with discrepancies between output and demand. So if inventories are high enough then demand may also be met by running down stocks when output has been set too low. Conversely, if production is greater than demand then stocks rise. If firms have a target level of stocks – in Program 9.2 it is 10 – then they will not only plan production to meet demand, but also to restore stock levels.

Line 100 in the program introduces the RESTORE statement. This moves the data-pointer back to the beginning of the DATA so that when the program is re-run at line 100 it can READ it again.

Program 9.2 Inventory/Stock model

```
    >
10 REM PROGRAM  STOCKS
20 REM NO  9.2
50 DEF FND(V)=INT(10*V+0.5)/10 : REM one decimal place
99 REM set initial values
100 RESTORE
```

```
110 READ ST,A,B,Z,Y
120 I=30
130 S=ST
199 REM input new values
200 PRINT "INCOME      = ";Y
210 PRINT "INVESTMENT = ";I
220 PRINT
230 PRINT "Input new investment ":
240 INPUT I
499 REM output results & calculate
500 PRINT
510 PRINT TAB(1);"PERIOD";TAB(10);"OUTPUT";TAB(20);"DEMAND";TAB(30);"STOCKS"
520 PRINT
530 FOR T= 1 TO 15
540 Z1=Z
550 Y1=Y
560 C=A+B*Y1
570 Z=C+I
580 Y=Z1+0.5*(ST-S)
590 S1=Y-Z
600 S=S+S1
610 IF S<0 THEN S=0
620 PRINT TAB(1);T;TAB(10);FND(Y);TAB(20);FND(Z);TAB(30);FND(S)
650 NEXT T
699 REM re-run option
700 PRINT
710 PRINT "1. To END program"
720 PRINT "2. To RUN it again"
730 INPUT R
740 IF R<1 OR R>2 THEN GOTO 730
750 IF R=2 THEN GOTO 100 : REM re-run
990 PRINT"END OF PROGRAM"
995 END
2998 REM stored data
2999 REM initial values for ST,A,B,Z,Y
3000 DATA 10,20,0.5,100,100

>
INCOME      = 100
INVESTMENT = 30

Input new investment ?40

PERIOD    OUTPUT    DEMAND    STOCKS

1         100       110       0
2         115       110       5
3         112.5     117.5     0
4         122.5     116.3     6.3
5         118.1     121.3     3.1
6         124.7     119.1     8.8
7         119.7     122.3     6.1
8         124.3     119.8     10.5
9         119.6     122.1     8
10        123.2     119.8     11.3
11        119.1     121.6     8.9
12        122.1     119.6     11.5
13        118.8     121.1     9.2
14        121.5     119.4     11.3
15        118.8     120.7     9.3

1. To END program
2. To RUN it again
?1
END OF PROGRAM
```

You will see from the sample run that raising investment by 10 does not produce the smooth response of the previous program. Instead output fluctuates around the static equilibrium of 120. Even after 15 periods firms have not achieved their desired stock level of 10. Of course, this is a simple model which does not credit firms with much ability to use past experience to predict future demand and plan output accordingly. On the other hand, the economy may be less stable than this model, as we shall see when we include the accelerator theory of investment.

9.4 The accelerator

So far we have assumed that investment is exogenous and unaffected by national income. When output rises it seems likely that this will encourage firms to invest more. The accelerator theory provides an explanation of this link. It is based on the view that there is a relationship between capital (plant and machinery) and output. If V is the capital output ratio (K/Y) and we assume this is the same as incremental ratio we have

$$V = \frac{\Delta K}{\Delta Y}$$

this can be rearranged

$$\Delta K = V.\Delta Y$$

as the ΔK is net investment (i.e. total spending on plant and machinery less the expenditure on replacement for worn-out or obsolete capital) then we can write the following relationship

$$I_t = V(Y_t - Y_{t-1})$$

Thus net investment spending depends on the *change* in income or output.

Program 9.3 Accelerator demonstration

```
 10 REM PROGRAM ACCELERATOR DEMONSTRATION
 20 REM NO   9.3
 50 DEF FND(X)=INT(10*X+0.5)/10 : REM one decimal place
 99 REM set initial values
100 V=1.5
110 D=30
120 I=30
130 Y=100
499 REM calculate & output results
500 PRINT TAB(1);"PERIOD";TAB(8);"INCOME";TAB(16);"INV'T";TAB(24);"Y DIFF"
(32);"I DIFF"
510 FOR T=0 TO 20
520 I1=I
530 Y1=Y
540 Y=100+20*SIN(T) : REM sine function, gives cyclical fluctuation
550 I=D+V*(Y-Y1)
560 PRINT TAB(1);T;TAB(8);FND(Y);TAB(16);FND(I);TAB(24);FND(Y-Y1);TAB(32);
I-I1)
600 NEXT T
650 PRINT
989 REM program end
990 PRINT "END OF PROGRAM"
995 END
```

```
>
PERIOD INCOME   INV'T    Y DIFF   I DIFF
0       100      30       0        0
1       116.8    55.2     16.8     25.2
2       118.2    32       1.4      -23.2
3       102.8    7        -15.4    -25.1
4       84.9     3.1      -18      -3.9
5       80.8     23.9     -4       20.9
6       94.4     50.4     13.6     26.4
7       113.1    58.1     18.7     7.7
8       119.8    40       6.6      -18.1
9       108.2    12.7     -11.5    -27.3
10      89.1     1.3      -19.1    -11.4
11      80       16.3     -9.1     15
12      89.3     43.9     9.3      27.6
13      108.4    58.7     19.1     14.8
14      119.8    47.1     11.4     -11.6
15      113      19.8     -6.8     -27.3
16      94.2     1.9      -18.8    -17.9
17      80.8     9.8      -13.5    7.9
18      85       36.3     4.2      26.5
19      103      57       18       20.7
20      118.3    52.9     15.3     -4.1

END OF PROGRAM
```

There are some interesting properties of this theory and Program 9.3 can be used to illustrate them. The program generates a cyclical fluctuation of income and shows how investment responds when V equals 1.5 and autonomous investment (part of investment spending that is unaffected by changes in income) is 30. Notice that fluctuations in investment are greater than those in income. As investment spending depends upon the change in income, it will fall if the increases in output get less. So before national income reaches a peak investment has started to decline. Similarly, investment starts to recover before the trough in output is reached. This illustration shows the effect of income on investment but, of course, investment also affects income with a multiplier effect. We combine these two effects in the next model.

9.5 Multiplier – accelerator model

Program 9.4 incorporates a lagged consumption function (from Program 9.1) and an accelerator relationship. The investment function is

$$I_t = D + V(Y_{t-1} - Y_{t-2})$$

which is a modified version of the one encountered in the previous section. As the sample run shows, you input the value of the MPC (B) and accelerator coefficient (V), and the equilibrium level of income for government spending is calculated. You then have an opportunity to input a new level of government expenditure. Income, consumption and investment are then calculated for 20 periods. You should try out different values of B and V.

Program 9.4 Multiplier–accelerator model

```
10 REM PROGRAM  MULTIPLIER-ACCELERATOR
20 REM NO   9.4
99 REM set initial values
100 A=20
110 D=10
120 G=10
125 N=0
199 REM input values & calculate
200 PRINT "INPUT MPC ";
210 INPUT B
220 PRINT "INPUT ACCELERATOR ";
230 INPUT V
240 Y=(A+D+G)/(1-B)
250 Y2=Y
260 Y1=Y
270 C=A+B*Y
280 I=D
290 PRINT
299 REM output initial position
300 GOSUB 1000 : REM table heading
310 GOSUB 1200 : REM fill table
349 REM input new value
350 PRINT
360 PRINT "INPUT NEW GOVERNMENT EXPENDITURE ";
370 INPUT G
499 REM calculate & output results
500 PRINT
510 GOSUB 1000 : REM table heading
520 FOR N=1 TO 30
530 Y2=Y1
540 Y1=Y
550 C=A+B*Y1
560 I=D+V*(Y1-Y2)
570 Y=C+I+G
580 GOSUB 1200 : REM fill table
600 IF N<>15 THEN GOTO 700
609 REM page results
610 PRINT
620 PRINT "Press <RETURN> to continue ";
630 INPUT Z$
640 PRINT
650 GOSUB 1000 : REM table heading
700 NEXT N
750 PRINT
989 REM program end
990 PRINT "END OF PROGRAM"
995 END
998 REM subroutines
999 REM table heading
1000 PRINT TAB(1);"TIME";TAB(10);"INCOME";TAB(20);"CONS'N";TAB(29);"INVESTM
1010 PRINT
1020 RETURN
1199 REM fill table
1200 PRINT TAB(1);N;TAB(10);INT (Y+.5);TAB(20);INT(C+.5);TAB(29);INT(I+.5)
1210 RETURN
```

```
>
INPUT MPC ?.5
INPUT ACCELERATOR ?1.5

TIME     INCOME     CONS'N    INVESTMENT

  0        80         60        10
```

```
INPUT NEW GOVERNMENT EXPENDITURE ?20

TIME        INCOME      CONS'N      INVESTMENT

1           90          60          10
2           110         65          25
3           135         75          40
4           155         88          48
5           158         98          40
6           133         99          14
7           79          86          -27
8           9           59          -71
9           -51         24          -95
10          -64         -5          -79
11          -3          -12         -11
12          141         19          102
13          336         90          226
14          511         188         303
15          567         275         272

Press <RETURN> to continue ?

TIME        INCOME      CONS'N      INVESTMENT

16          419         304         95
17          36          229         -213
18          -506        38          -564
19          -1015       -233        -803
20          -1223       -488        -755
21          -872        -591        -301
22          140         -416        536
23          1638        90          1528
24          3116        839         2257
25          3825        1578        2227
26          3026        1932        1073
27          365         1533        -1188
28          -3760       202         -3982
29          -8016       -1860       -6176
30          -10343      -3988       -6375

END OF PROGRAM
```

You should discover that several cases can occur, depending on the values of B and V. Fluctuations may be explosive, dampened or continuous. You would get no fluctuations with certain combinations, with output behaving as it did in Program 9.1 or, if B and V are sufficiently high, income would rise indefinitely.

This program can be used with the graphic sub-routine listed in the Appendix. The routine will produce a graph of the movements in income over 30 time periods. The following lines should be added to Program 9.4:

```
60 DIM Y(30)
130 Y$="INCOME"
140 MT=30
245 Y(0)=Y
575 Y(N)=Y
800 PRINT "PRESS RETURN FOR GRAPH"
810 INPUT R$
820 GOSUB 2000
```

9.6 Stabilization policy

The history of market economies suggests they suffer from cyclical fluctuations. The multiplier-accelerator relationship is one of many theories that have been offered as an explanation of this behaviour. In this section we use the model to illustrate the problem facing governments who attempt to reduce these fluctuations.

In Program 9.5 you have to adjust government spending to try to achieve a target level of income of 100. Government expenditure has been raised to 20 prior to your appointment as Chancellor. The model predicts that output will fluctuate around 100 (approximately from 78 to 122) if government spending is maintained at 20. You cannot affect output in the current period but government expenditure does affect it in the next – reflecting the time lag between a government's decision to change policy and its policy starting to have an effect. After 10 years the program calculates how successful you have been. It shows how much of the cycle that would have occurred if no policy changes were made (that is, government spending had remained at 20) has been dampened or reduced. A negative figure indicates fluctuations have been made worse. The OECD, in a study of fiscal policy in the 1950s and 60s which used a similar measure to gauge the effect of policy, found a figure of −13% for the UK, which you might find reassuring if you fail to achieve 100% dampening after a few attempts.

Program 9.5 Stabilization policy

```
 10 REM PROGRAM   STABILISE
 20 REM NO  9.5
 99 REM set initial values
100 RESTORE
110 READ A,B,D,V,G
120 READ S
130 Y=80
140 Y1=80
150 SS=2081^0.5
199 REM input value & calculate
200 FOR T=1 TO 10
210 Y2=Y1
220 Y1=Y
230 C=A+B*Y1
240 I=D+V*(Y1-Y2)
250 Y=C+I+G
260 S=S+(100-Y)^2
270 PRINT "NATIONAL INCOME IN YEAR ";T;" IS ";INT(Y*10+0.5)/10
280 PRINT
290 PRINT"Input new government expenditure ";
300 INPUT G
310 PRINT
320 PRINT
400 NEXT T
499 REM output final result
```

```
500 PRINT
510 S=S^0.5
520 ST=INT(((SS-S)/SS)*100)+0.5)
530 PRINT "% OF CYCLE DAMPENED WAS ";ST
540 IF ST>0 THEN PRINT "Fluctuations reduced"
550 IF ST<0 THEN PRINT "Fluctuations made worse"
560 IF ST=0 THEN PRINT "Fluctuations not reduced"
699 REM re-run option
700 PRINT
710 PRINT "1. To END program"
720 PRINT "2. To RUN it again"
730 INPUT R
740 IF R<1 OR R>2 THEN GOTO 730
750 IF R=2 THEN GOTO 100 : REM re-run
989 REM program end
990 PRINT"END OF PROGRAM"
995 END
2998 REM stored data
2999 REM initial values for A,B,D,V,G
3000 DATA 20,0.5,10,1,20
3009 REM initial value for S
3010 DATA 0


?

>RUN
NATIONAL INCOME IN YEAR 1 IS 90

Input new government expenditure ?10


NATIONAL INCOME IN YEAR 2 IS 95

Input new government expenditure ?5
.
.
.
.
.

% OF CYCLE DAMPENED WAS 46
Fluctuations reduced

1. To END program
2. To RUN it again
?1
END OF PROGRAM
```

9.7 Investment and growth

Keynes's model concentrated on the effect of investment as a
component of demand on output. Pessimism by businessmen may
result in low investment and the failure of the economy to operate
at full capacity with low unemployment levels. But investment also
affects capacity as well as capacity utilization. Net investment
raises the capital stock and we would expect that to raise the
output the economy is capable of producing. So investment has a
dual effect: it affects output and capacity. Program 9.6 allows you
to explore this relationship. You will find that investment needs to
grow to maintain full employment. This leads us into the issue of
growth, which we consider briefly in the next section.

Program 9.6 Domar and investment

>

```
10 REM PROGRAM  DOMAR
20 REM NO  9.6
99 REM set initial values
100 A=20
110 B=.5
120 V=2
130 I=30
140 YF=(A+I)/(1-B)
299 REM calculate
300 Y=(A+I)/(1-B)
310 YF=YF+(I/V)
499 REM output results
500 PRINT "INCOME ";Y
510 PRINT "F.E INCOME ";YF
520 PRINT "INVESTMENT ";I
530 PRINT
599 REM input new value
600 PRINT "INPUT NEW INVESTMENT (-1 to END) ";
610 INPUT I
620 IF I=-1 THEN GOTO 990 : REM end
640 PRINT
650 GOTO 300 : REM re-calculate
989 REM program end
990 PRINT"END OF PROGRAM"
995 END
```

>

```
INCOME 100
F.E INCOME 115
INVESTMENT 30

INPUT NEW INVESTMENT (-1 to END) ?40

INCOME 120
F.E INCOME 135
INVESTMENT 40

INPUT NEW INVESTMENT (-1 to END) ?-1
END OF PROGRAM
```

9.8 A simple growth model

It did not take long after the publication of the 'General Theory' for economists to explore the implications for growth of the basic Keynesian model. Domar, in the 1940s, investigated the issue we considered in the previous section – the rate of growth of investment necessary to maintain full employment. Harrod, in the late 1930s, retained Keynes's doubts about the ability of market economies to achieve and maintain full employment when he placed the income-expenditure model in a growth setting. We can see the reason for this if we take a simple model where the equilibrium condition is

$$I = S$$

with a simple savings function

$$S = sY$$

and the relationship between investment and changes in output discussed in the section on the accelerator

$$I = V.\Delta Y$$

we get

$$V.\Delta Y = sY$$

rearranging

$$\frac{\Delta Y}{Y} = \frac{s}{V}$$

where the term on the left hand side is the growth rate.

Harrod called this the warranted growth rate (GW). We now consider another concept, the natural growth rate (GN):

$$GN = N + Q$$

This is the growth rate which would be required to give full employment, because N is the growth in the labour supply and Q the growth in productivity. To maintain full employment the warranted rate needs to be equal to the natural rate:

$$\frac{S}{V} = N + Q$$

Harrod's pessimism arose from what he considered to be the independent nature of these variables. For example, s (the marginal propensity to save) depended on the behaviour of households and N depended on demographic factors.

There is a further problem that Harrod revealed. This is concerned with whether the actual rate of growth (GA) will equal the warranted rate. If the two are not equal then they will tend to move further away from each other.

Program 9.7 Harrod growth model

```
>
  10 REM PROGRAM  HARROD
  20 REM NO  9.7
  50 DEF FND(V)=INT(10*V+0.5)/10 : REM one decimal place
  99 REM set initial values
 100 LS=10
 110 Y=100
 120 N=0.03
 130 Q=0.02
 140 GN=N+Q
 150 LD=10
 160 U=LS-LD
 199 REM input new values
 200 PRINT "OUTPUT ";Y
```

```
210 PRINT "UNEMPLOYMENT ";U
220 PRINT
230 PRINT "INPUT S ";
240 INPUT S
250 PRINT "INPUT V ";
260 INPUT V
270 GW=(S/V)
280 GA=GW
290 PRINT
300 PRINT "WARRANTED GROWTH RATE ";GW*100
310 PRINT "NATURAL GROWTH RATE   ";GN*100
320 PRINT "Input expected growth rate ";
330 INPUT GE
340 GE=GE/100
499 REM output results
500 PRINT
510 PRINT TAB(1);"YR";TAB(4);"GN";TAB(7);"GW";TAB(11);"GA";TAB(19);"GE";TA
B);"UNEMP'T";TAB(33);"OUTPUT"
520 PRINT
530 FOR T=1 TO 5
540 Y1=Y
550 I=V*((Y1/(1-GE))-Y1)
560 Y=I/S
570 IF Y<1 THEN Y=1
580 GA=INT(((Y-Y1)/Y)*1000+.5)/1000 : REM to three decimal places
590 LS=LS*(1+N)
600 LD=LD*(1+GA-Q)
610 U=LS-LD
620 PRINT TAB(1);T;TAB(4);FND(GN*100);TAB(7);FND(GW*100);TAB(11);FND(GA*10
AB(19);FND(GE*100);TAB(25);FND(U);TAB(33);FND(Y)
630 GE=(GE+0.05*(GA-GE))
650 NEXT T
699 REM re-run option
700 PRINT
710 PRINT "1. To END program"
720 PRINT "2. To RUN it again"
730 INPUT R
740 IF R<1 OR R>2 THEN GOTO 730
750 IF R=2 THEN GOTO 100 : REM re-run
989 REM program end
990 PRINT "END OF PROGRAM"
995 END
```

```
OUTPUT 100
UNEMPLOYMENT 0

INPUT S ?.2
INPUT V ?2

WARRANTED GROWTH RATE 10
NATURAL GROWTH RATE    5
Input expected growth rate ?9

 YR GN GW   GA     GE    UNEMP'T OUTPUT

 1  5  10  -1.1    9     0.6     98.9
 2  5  10  -7.7    8.5   1.9     91.8
 3  5  10  -20.1   7.7   4.1     76.4
 4  5  10  -48.8   6.3   7.9     51.4
 5  5  10  -172.4  3.5   14.1    18.9

1. To END program
2. To RUN it again
?1
END OF PROGRAM
```

The 'instability' problem (whether $GN = GA$) and the 'uniqueness' problem (whether $GW = GN$) are illustrated in Program 9.7. The sample run particularly highlights the former problem. If businessmen estimate a growth rate less than the warranted rate they achieve a growth rate less than the one they expected. Believing they overestimated, they revise downwards their investment plans resulting in a still lower growth rate. The warranted rate is the only that, when it is expected, will be achieved.

9.9 The IS–LM model

We turn now to an attempt to integrate some aspects of the Keynesian income expenditure model with those theories which stress the importance of the money supply.

If we extend the basic Keynesian model to allow investment to be influenced by the rate of interest, then we find that we have a different equilibrium income level for each interest rate. Program 9.8 allows you to explore this relationship.

Program 9.8 IS schedule model

```
 10 REM PROGRAM  INTEREST
 20 REM NO  9.8
 99 REM set initial values
100 READ A,B,D,V,G
110 R=10
299 REM calculate
300 Y=(A+D+G+V*R)/(1-B)
310 I=D+V*R
499 REM output results
500 PRINT "EQUILIBRIUM INCOME = ";Y
510 PRINT "INVESTMENT         = ";I
520 PRINT "RATE OF INTEREST   = ";R
530 PRINT
599 REM input new value
600 PRINT "Input new interest rate (-1 to END) ";
610 INPUT R
620 IF R=-1 THEN GOTO 990 : REM end
630 GOTO 300 : REM re-calculate
989 REM program end
990 PRINT "END OF PROGRAM"
995 END
2998 REM stored data
2999 REM initial values for A,B,D,V,G
3000 DATA 20,0.5,25,-1,15
```

```
>
EQUILIBRIUM INCOME = 100
INVESTMENT         = 15
RATE OF INTEREST   = 10

Input new interest rate (-1 to END) ?5
EQUILIBRIUM INCOME = 110
INVESTMENT         = 20
RATE OF INTEREST   = 5

Input new interest rate (-1 to END) ?-1
END OF PROGRAM
```

You should find that lower interest rates lead to higher investment spending which raises both aggregate and the equilibrium level of income. If you plot the results you get from the program you will find the relationship illustrated below. The line is called the IS schedule and shows points of equilibrium in what is often described as the 'product market'.

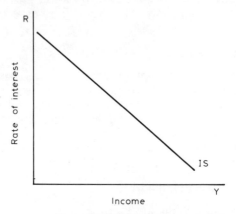

Figure 9.2 The IS schedule

We can also refer to a 'money market'. Equilibrium here is where the money supply (which is assumed to be exogenous) is equal to the demand for money.

The demand for money is likely to be affected by two factors. First, higher incomes will generally mean people wish to hold more money. Secondly, interest rates are likely to affect the demand for money because at higher rates people will generally hold less money and hold more government bonds or building society deposits.

The relationship is shown below in Figure 9.3 and is illustrated in Program 9.9. Run the program with constant income levels and see the effects of changes in the money supply. You should find that increases in money supply lower interest rates. Now run the program with a constant money supply but vary the income level. You will find the higher income levels cause higher interest rates. This is because the demand for money is raised when income increases, but with a fixed money supply higher interest rates must occur if equilibrium is to be maintained in the money market. If you plot this relationship you obtain a line, called the LM schedule, which is illustrated in Figure 9.4. This shows points of equilibrium in the money market.

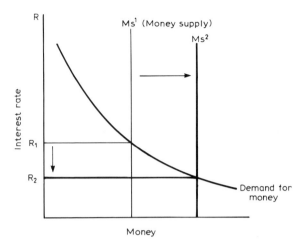

Figure 9.3 The money market

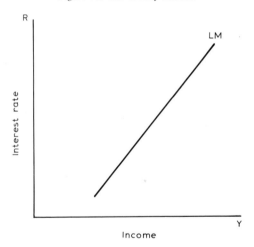

Figure 9.4 The LM schedule

Program 9.9 LM schedule model

```
10 REM PROGRAM
20 REM NO  9.9
99 REM set initial values
100 READ S,K,U,Y,M
299 REM calculate
300 R=(M-S)/U-(K*Y)/U
499 REM output results
500 PRINT
```

```
510 PRINT "INTEREST RATE   = ";R
520 PRINT "MONEY SUPPLY    = ";M
530 PRINT "INCOME          = ";Y
540 PRINT
599 REM input new values
600 PRINT "Input new money supply (-1 to END) ";
610 INPUT M
620 IF M=-1 THEN GOTO 990 : REM end
630 PRINT "Input new income ";
640 INPUT Y
680 GOTO 300 : REM re-calculate
989 REM program end
990 PRINT "END OF PROGRAM"
995 END
2998 REM stored data
2999 REM initial values for S,K,U,Y,M
3000 DATA 10,0.25,-1,100,25


>

INTEREST RATE   = 10
MONEY SUPPLY    = 25
INCOME          = 100

Input new money supply (-1 to END) ?25
Input new income ?120

INTEREST RATE   = 15
MONEY SUPPLY    = 25
INCOME          = 120

Input new money supply (-1 to END) ?-1
END OF PROGRAM
```

We have now established the basis of the link between product and money markets. In the former the equilibrium level of income depends upon the rate of interest, and this is determined in the money market.

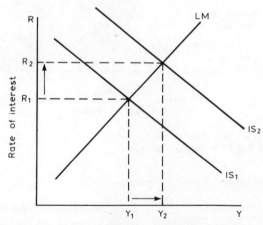

Figure 9.5 The IS-LM model showing the effect of an increase in government expenditure

Program 9.10 calculates the equilibrium income level and interest rate. As the sample run shows an increase in government spending raises the level of income as Keynesians would expect. But this raises the demand for money which increases interest rates which have an effect on investment spending so the government expenditure multiplier will not normally be as large as the one obtained in the income expenditure model found in Chapter 7.

The general solution, where both product and money markets are in equilibrium, is shown graphically in Figure 9.5. Also it is used in our final program.

Program 9.10 IS–LM model

```
10 REM PROGRAM  IS-LM MODEL
20 REM NO  9.10
50 DEF FND(X)=INT(10*X+0.5)/10 : REM one decimal place
99 REM set initial values
100 RESTORE
110 READ S,K,U,M
120 READ A,B,D,V,G
140 I=10
150 J=1
299 REM calculate
310 Y=(A+D+G-(V/U)*(S-M))/((1-B)+(V*K)/U) :REM equilibrium condition
320 R=(M-S)/U-(K*Y)/U
330 I=D+V*R
469 REM output results
470 PRINT
480 PRINT "YEAR ";J
500 PRINT
510 PRINT "INCOME         = ";FND(Y)
520 PRINT "INTEREST RATE  = ";FND(R)
530 PRINT "MONEY SUPPLY   = ";FND(M)
540 PRINT "GOVERNMENT EXP.= ";FND(G)
580 PRINT
599 REM input new values
600 PRINT "Input new money supply (-1 to END) ";
610 INPUT M
620 IF M=-1 THEN GOTO 700 : REM re-run?
630 PRINT "Input new government expenditure    ";
640 INPUT G
670 J=J+1 : REM increment year
680 GOTO 310 : REM re-calculate
699 REM re-run option
700 PRINT
710 PRINT "1. To END program"
720 PRINT "2. To RUN it again"
730 INPUT RR : REM 'R' already used
740 IF RR<1 OR RR>2 THEN GOTO 730
780 IF RR=2 THEN GOTO 100 : REM re-run
989 REM program end
990 PRINT "END OF PROGRAM"
995 END
2998 REM stored data
2999 REM initial values for S,K,U,M
3000 DATA 10,0.25,-1,25
3009 REM initial values for A,B,D,V,G
3010 DATA 20,0.5,25,-1,15
```

```
> RUN

YEAR 1

INCOME          = 100
INTEREST RATE   = 10
MONEY SUPPLY    = 25
GOVERNMENT EXP. = 15

Input new money supply (-1 to END)  ?25
Input new government expenditure     ?25

YEAR 2

INCOME          = 113.3
INTEREST RATE   = 13.3
MONEY SUPPLY    = 25
GOVERNMENT EXP. = 25

Input new money supply (-1 to END)  ?20
Input new government expenditure     ?25

YEAR 3

INCOME          = 106.7
INTEREST RATE   = 16.7
MONEY SUPPLY    = 20
GOVERNMENT EXP. = 25

Input new money supply (-1 to END)  ?-1

1. To END program
2. To RUN it again
?1
END OF PROGRAM
```

9.10 Policy model

Program 9.11 tries to include a number of features of our extended
macro model which we have covered in this chapter. It is an
IS–LM model with taxation included. So you can use fiscal policy,
changing government expenditure and tax rates, to alter national
income but you will find that monetary policy, changing the money
supply is important too. The program includes an aspect of our
earlier discussion in this chapter, because investment affects full
employment output, or capacity, of the economy. Capacity grows
by 1% per annum, reflecting changing technology, plus an amount
that depends upon investment in the previous period. Unemployment is related to how close output is to capacity. There are many
further features that could be added – inflation, imports and
exports, supply-side effects. But that is the exciting feature of
macro models – they are never complete. By now you should have
gained some insights into economic model building, with the aid of
a computer and this book, so that your appetite has been whetted
to read and experiment more.

Program 9.11 Policy model

```
10 REM PROGRAM  POLICY MODEL
20 REM NO  9.11
50 DEF FND(X)=INT(10*X+0.5)/10 : REM one decimal place
99 REM set initial values
100 RESTORE
110 READ S,K,U,M,T
120 READ A,B,D,V,G
130 YF=98
140 I=10
150 J=1
299 REM calculate
300 YF=YF*(1+0.01)+(I/10)
310 Y=(A+D+G-(V/U)*(S-M))/((1-B*(1-T))+(V*K)/U)
320 R=(M-S)/U-(K*Y)/U
330 I=D+V*R
340 UT=5+(YF-Y)
350 IF UT<3 THEN UT=3
469 REM output results
470 PRINT
480 PRINT "YEAR ";J
490 PRINT
500 PRINT "CAPACITY         = ";FND(YF)
510 PRINT "INCOME           = ";FND(Y)
520 PRINT "INTEREST RATE    = ";FND(R)
530 PRINT "MONEY SUPPLY     = ";FND(M)
540 PRINT "GOVERNMENT EXP.= ";FND(G)
550 PRINT "TAX REVENUE      = ";FND(T*Y)
560 PRINT "TAX RATE         = ";FND(T)
570 PRINT "UNEMPLOYMENT(%)= ";FND(UT)
580 PRINT
599 REM input new values
600 PRINT "Input new money supply (-1 to END) ";
610 INPUT M
620 IF M=-1 THEN GOTO 700 : REM re-run?
630 PRINT "Input new government expenditure    ";
640 INPUT G
650 PRINT "Input new tax rate                  ";
660 INPUT T
670 J=J+1 : REM increment year
680 GOTO 300 : REM re-calculate
699 REM re-run option
700 PRINT
710 PRINT "1. To END program"
720 PRINT "2. To RUN it again"
730 INPUT RR : REM 'R' already used
740 IF RR<1 OR RR>2 THEN GOTO 730
780 IF RR=2 THEN GOTO 100 : REM re-run
989 REM program end
990 PRINT "END OF PROGRAM"
995 END
2998 REM stored data
2999 REM initial values for S,K,U,M,T
3000 DATA 10,0.25,-1,25,0.2
3009 REM initial values for A,B,D,V,G
3010 DATA 20,0.5,25,-1,15
```

```
YEAR 1

CAPACITY         = 100
INCOME           = 88.2
INTEREST RATE    = 7.1
MONEY SUPPLY     = 25
GOVERNMENT EXP.= 15
TAX REVENUE      = 17.6
TAX RATE         = 0.2
UNEMPLOYMENT(%)= 16.7
```

```
Input new money supply (-1 to END)  ?25
Input new government expenditure     ?30
Input new tax rate                   ?.2

YEAR 2

CAPACITY          = 102.8
INCOME            = 105.9
INTEREST RATE     = 11.5
MONEY SUPPLY      = 25
GOVERNMENT EXP.   = 30
TAX REVENUE       = 21.2
TAX RATE          = 0.2
UNEMPLOYMENT(%)   = 3

Input new money supply (-1 to END)  ?-1

1. To END program
2. To RUN it again
?1
END OF PROGRAM
```

EXERCISES

(9.1) Using program 9.4 on the multiplier accelerator, choose a value for the marginal propensity to consume (e.g. equal to 0.5) and select different values of the accelerator coefficient ranging from 0 to 4, in steps of 0.5, and examine the pattern of output you obtain. Can you explain the different patterns?

(9.2) Program 9.4 may produce a negative level of income which is clearly unrealistic. Adapt the program to introduce a 'floor' to the fall in income. You may also introduce a 'ceiling' to reflect the full employment level of income.

(9.3) Adapt Program 9.10 to introduce time-lags. For example, incorporate a lag between the interest rate and investment, and between income and the demand for money.

(9.4) Program 9.11 may be developed in a number of ways as the text suggests. Introduce the accelerator and the lagged consumption function. Exports and imports and the balance of payments position could be added. For the more adventurous, introduce inflation using a Phillips-curve relationship, but consider carefully the effects this has on the monetary sector.

Appendix

Graphics sub-routine

The sub-routine presented below produces a line graph of the value of a variable over time. The time period is specified by dimensioning the array Y(T) with the value for the time period T.

Using the sub-routine will enhance the Cobweb Program 3.4, and the Multiplier–Accelerator Program 9.4. Versions are provided for three micro-computers in common use: the BBC, RML 380/480Z, and Apple II. It is suggested that you type in the appropriate program for your machine and save it on disc ready to use. The routine should be loaded into memory *before* typing in Programs 3.4 and 9.4. In order to link each program into the graphics routine it will be necessary to enter the additional lines described in each chapter.

Notes on particular versions

Apple II version

The graph on the Apple version has no labelling. If you wish to label the axes, it will be necessary to add your own program routine after line 2900 to:

PLOT TEXT Z$ AT XG,YG

where XG, YG are the coordinates of the first text character.

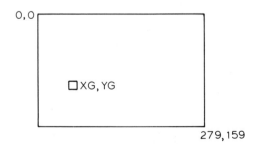

```
1995  REM  >>> graphics subroutine <<<
1996  REM  graph variable Y$ with values Y(t) against t
1997  REM  must DIM Y(30) in the program, store values in array and set Y$
1998  REM  and set MT=10 or MT=30 , the top of the time scale
1999  REM  calculate max & min values
2000  MY = 10
2010  NY = 0
2020  NT = 0
2030  FOR IG = NT TO MT
2040  IF Y(IG) > MY THEN MY = Y(IG): REM   max
2050  IF Y(IG) < NY THEN NY = Y(IG): REM   min
2060  NEXT IG
2069  REM  scale to nearest ten
2070  NY = 10 * INT (NY / 10)
2080  IF MY < > 10 * INT (MY / 10) THEN MY = 10 * INT (MY / 10) + 10
2088  REM  scale ... time NT to MT
2089  REM              variable Y$  NY to MY
2099  REM  set graphics
2100  TEXT
2105  HOME
2110  HGR
2119  REM  set colours
2120  HCOLOR= 3: REM  colour 3 = white
2199  REM  draw graph axes & grid
2200  HPLOT 70,20 TO 70,140: REM  draw line from (70,20) to (70,140)
2205  HPLOT  TO 250,140
2220  HCOLOR= 2: REM  colour 2 = purple
2229  REM  draw grid
2230  FOR IG = 1 TO 10
2240  HPLOT 70 + IG * 18,140 TO 70 + IG * 18,20
2250  HPLOT 70,140 - IG * 12 TO 250,140 - IG * 12
2295  NEXT IG
2299  REM  label axes
2300  Z$ = Y$:XG = 70:YG = 16: GOSUB 2900: REM   plot text
2305  XG = 150:YG = 158:Z$ = "time": GOSUB 2900
2309  REM  time axis
2310  Z$ =  STR$ (NT): REM  convert number NT to string Z$
2315  XG = 66:YG = 149: GOSUB 2900
2320  Z$ =  STR$ (MT):XG = 242: GOSUB 2900
2325  IF MT - NT < > 5 * INT ((MT - NT) / 5) THEN 2350: REM  label Y axis
2329  REM  label more divisions
2330  FOR IG = 2 TO 8 STEP 2
2335  Z$ =  STR$ (NT + IG * (MT - NT) / 10)
2339  REM  LEN(Z$) .. length of string Z$ , (number of characters)
2340  XG = 70 + 18 * IG - 4 * LEN (Z$): GOSUB 2900
2345  NEXT IG
2347  REM  label Y axis
2350  FOR IG = 0 TO 10
2355  Z$ =  STR$ (NY + IG * (MY - NY) / 10)
2360  XG = 66 - 7 * LEN (Z$):YG = 144 - IG * 12: GOSUB 2900
2365  NEXT IG
2399  REM  plot points
2400  FOR IG = NT TO MT
2405  HCOLOR= 3: REM  white
2410  IF IG = NT THEN HPLOT 70,140 - 120 * (Y(IG) - NY) / (MY - NY): REM  plot
first point
2415  HPLOT  TO 70 + 180 * (IG - NT) / (MT - NT),140 - 120 * (Y(IG) - NY) / (MY
- NY): REM  draw to next
2450  NEXT IG
2499  REM  select option
2500  HOME : VTAB 21: REM  clear text screen
2510  PRINT "  Choose    1 Alter scales"
2515  PRINT "            2 Return to program"
2520  PRINT
2525  PRINT "            Which (1 or 2)";
2530  INPUT WG
2535  IF WG < 1 OR WG > 2 OR WG < > INT (WG) THEN 2500: REM  re-input
2550  IF WG = 2 THEN 2790: REM  return to program
2599  REM  alter scales
2600  HOME : VTAB 21: REM  clear text screen
2610  PRINT "  Minimum time ( 0 - 30 ) ";
2615  INPUT NT
2620  PRINT
2625  PRINT "  Maximum time (";NT;" - 30 ) ";
2630  INPUT MT
2635  IF NT < 0 OR (MT < = NT) OR MT > 30 THEN 2600: REM   re-input
2649  REM  alter Y scale
2650  HOME : VTAB 21: REM  clear text screen
2655  PRINT "  Minimum value of ";Y$;" ";
```

```
2665  INPUT NY
2670  PRINT
2675  PRINT "  Maximum value of ";Y$;" ";
2680  INPUT MY
2690  GOTO 2030: REM  re-calculate / re-draw
2789  REM  re-set screen
2790  TEXT
2792  HOME
2800  RETURN
2899  REM  subroutine plot text Z$ at (XG,YG)
2900  REM ...INSERT YOUR OWN ROUTINE HERE !
2901  REM ...IT IS NOT POSSIBLE TO COMBINE TEXT & GRAPHICS IN STANDARD APPLE BAS
IC
2925  RETURN
```

RML 380/480Z

The RML sub-routine requires the following version of BASIC:

BASICSG2

(i.e. graphics level 2)

```
1995 REM >>> graphics subroutine <<<
1996 REM graph variable Y$ with values Y(t) against t
1997 REM must DIM Y(30) in the program, store values in array and set Y$
1998 REM and set MT=10 or MT=30 , the top of the time scale
1999 REM calculate max & min values
2000 MY=10
2010 NY=0
2020 NT=0
2030 FOR IG=NT TO MT
2040 IF Y(IG)>MY THEN MY=Y(IG) : REM max
2050 IF Y(IG)<NY THEN NY=Y(IG) : REM min
2060 NEXT IG
2069 REM scale to nearest ten
2070 NY=10*INT(NY/10)
2080 IF MY<>10*INT(MY/10) THEN MY=10*INT(MY/10)+10
2088 REM scale ... time NT to MT
2089 REM            variable Y$  NY to MY
2099 REM set graphics
2100 TEXT
2105 PUT 12,29
2110 GRAPH
2115 CALL "RESOLUTION",0,2
2119 REM set colours
2120 CALL "COLOUR",0,255 : REM colour 0 = white
2125 CALL "COLOUR",1,0   : REM colour 1 = black
2130 CALL "COLOUR",2,200 : REM colour 2 = yellow
2135 CALL "COLOUR",3,64  : REM colour 3 = red
2199 REM draw graph axes & grid
2200 CALL "PLOT",80,175,1 : CALL "LINE",80,25 : REM draw line from (80,175) to (
80,25) , in colour 1 = black
2205 CALL "LINE",280,25
2229 REM draw grid
2230 FOR IG=1 TO 10
2240 CALL "PLOT",80+IG*20,25,1 : REM black
2245 CALL "LINE",80+IG*20,26
2250 CALL "PLOT",80,25+IG*15,1
2255 CALL "LINE",81,25+IG*15
2269 REM yellow grid
2275 CALL "PLOT",80+IG*20,27,2 : REM yellow
2280 CALL "LINE",80+IG*20,175
2285 CALL "PLOT",82,25+IG*15,2
2290 CALL "LINE",280,25+IG*15
2295 NEXT IG
2299 REM label axes
2300 Z$=Y$ : XG=80 : YG=180 : GOSUB 2900 : REM plot text
2305 XG=165 : YG=2 : Z$="time" : GOSUB 2900
2309 REM time axis
2310 Z$=STR$(NT) : REM convert number NT to string Z$
2315 XG=67 : YG=14 : GOSUB 2900
```

```
2320 Z$=STR$(MI) : XG=264 : GOSUB 2900
2325 IF MI-NT<>5*INT((MI-NT)/5) THEN 2350 : REM label Y axis
2329 REM label more divisions
2330 FOR IG=2 TO 8 STEP 2
2335 Z$=STR$(NI+IG*(MI-NI)/10)
2339 REM LEN(Z$) .. length of string Z$ , (number of characters)
2340 XG=76+20*IG-4*LEN(Z$) : GOSUB 2900
2345 NEXT IG
2349 REM label Y axis
2350 FOR IG=0 TO 10
2355 Z$=STR$(NY+IG*(MY-NY)/10)
2360 XG=74-8*LEN(Z$) : YG=21+IG*15 : GOSUB 2900
2365 NEXT IG
2399 REM plot points
2400 FOR IG=NT TO MI
2405 REM colour 3 = red
2410 IF IG=NT THEN CALL "PLOT",80,25+150*(Y(IG)-NY)/(MY-NY),3 : REM plot first p
oint
2415 CALL "LINE",80+200*(IG-NT)/(MI-NT),25+150*(Y(IG)-NY)/(MY-NY) : REM draw to
next
2450 NEXT IG
2499 REM select option
2500 PUT 12,29 : REM clear text screen
2510 PRINT " Choose    1 Alter scales"
2515 PRINT "            2 Return to program"
2520 PRINT
2525 PRINT "              Which (1 or 2)";
2530 INPUT WG
2535 IF WG<1 OR WG>2 OR WG<>INT(WG) THEN 2500 : REM re-input
2550 IF WG=2 THEN 2790 : REM return to program
2599 REM alter scales
2600 PUT 12,29 : REM clear screen
2610 PRINT " Minimum time ( 0 - 30 ) ";
2615 INPUT NT
2620 PRINT
2625 PRINT " Maximum time (";NT;" - 30 ) ";
2630 INPUT MT
2635 IF NT<0 OR MT<=NT OR MT>30 THEN 2600 : REM re-input
2649 REM alter Y scale
2650 PUT 12,29 : REM clear screen
2655 PRINT " Minimum value of ";Y$;" ";
2665 INPUT NY
2670 PRINT
2675 PRINT " Maximum value of ";Y$;" ";
2680 INPUT MY
2690 GOTO 2030 : REM re-calculate / re-draw
2789 REM re-set screen
2790 TEXT
2792 PUT ,12,29
2794 CALL "RESOLUTION",0,2
2800 RETURN
2899 REM subroutine plot text Z$ at (XG,YG)
2900 CALL "STPLOT",XG,YG,VARADR(Z$),1 : REM black
2925 RETURN
```

BBC

```
1995 REM >>> graphics subroutine <<<
1996 REM graph variable Y$ with values Y(t) against t
1997 REM must DIM Y(30) in program, store values in array and set Y$
1998 REM and set MT=10 or MT=30 , the top of the time scale
1999 REM calculate max & min values
2000 MY=10
2010 NY=0
2020 NT=0
2030 FOR IG=NT TO MT
2040 IF Y(IG)>MY THEN MY=Y(IG) : REM max
2050 IF Y(IG)<NY THEN NY=Y(IG) : REM min
2060 NEXT IG
2069 REM scale to nearest ten
2070 NY=10*INT(NY/10)
2080 IF MY<>10*INT(MY/10) THEN MY=10*INT(MY/10)+10
2088 REM scale .. time NT to MT
2089 REM          variable Y$ NY to MY
```

```
2099 REM set graphics
2100 MODE 1
2105 VDU24,0;0;1212;1000; : REM graphics window
2110 GCOL 0,131
2115 CLG : REM set graph area to white
2120 VDU 28,0,4,37,0 : REM text window
2125 COLOUR 129
2130 CLS : REM set text area to red
2135 COLOUR 2 : REM write text in yellow
2199 REM draw graph axes & grid
2200 GCOL 0,0 : REM colour black
2205 MOVE 300,800
2210 DRAW 300,100 : REM draw from (300,800) to (300,100)
2215 DRAW 1000,100 : REM draw to (1000,100)
2229 REM grid
2230 FOR IG=1 TO 10
2235 GCOL 0,0 : REM black axis marking
2240 MOVE 300+IG*70,100
2245 DRAW 300+IG*70,104
2250 MOVE 300,100+IG*70
2255 DRAW 304,100+IG*70
2269 REM yellow grid
2270 GCOL 0,2 : REM yellow
2275 MOVE 300+IG*70,108
2280 DRAW 300+IG*70,800
2285 MOVE 308,100+IG*70
2290 DRAW 1000,100+IG*70
2295 NEXT IG
2299 REM label axes
2300 Z$=Y$ : XG=300 : YG=844 : GOSUB 2900 : REM plot text
2305 XG=600 : YG=40 : Z$="time" : GOSUB 2900
2309 REM time axis
2310 Z$=STR$(NT) : REM convert number NT to string Z$
2315 XG=280 : YG=84 : GOSUB 2900
2320 Z$=STR$(MT) : XG=968 : GOSUB 2900
2325 IF MT-NT<>5*INT((MT-NT)/5) THEN 2350 : REM label Y axis
2329 REM label more divisions
2330 FOR IG=2 TO 8 STEP 2
2335 Z$=STR$(NT+IG*(MT-NT)/10)
2339 REM LEN(Z$) .. length of string Z$ , (number of characters).
2340 XG=300+70*IG-16*LEN(Z$) : GOSUB 2900
2345 NEXT IG
2349 REM label Y axis
2350 FOR IG=0 TO 10
2355 Z$=STR$(NY+IG*(MY-NY)/10)
2360 XG=276-32*LEN(Z$) : YG=112+IG*70 : GOSUB 2900
2365 NEXT IG
2399 REM plot points
2400 FOR IG=NT TO MT
2405 GCOL 0,1 : REM colour red
2410 IF IG=NT THEN MOVE 300,100+700*(Y(IG)-NY)/(MY-NY) : REM plot first point
2420 DRAW 300+700*(IG-NT)/(MT-NT),100+700*(Y(IG)-NY)/(MY-NY) : REM draw to next
point
2450 NEXT IG
2499 REM select option
2500 CLS : REM clear text
2505 PRINT
2510 PRINT " Choose   1 Alter scales"
2515 PRINT "          2 Return to program"
2520 PRINT
2525 PRINT "              Which (1 or 2)";
2530 INPUT WG
2535 IF WG<1 OR WG>2 OR WG<>INT(WG) THEN 2500 : REM re-input
2550 IF WG=2 THEN 2790 : REM return to program
2599 REM alter scales
2600 CLS : REM clear screen
2605 PRINT
2610 PRINT " Minimum time (0-30) ";
2615 INPUT NT
2620 PRINT
2625 PRINT " Maximum time (";NT;"-30) ";
2630 INPUT MT
2635 IF NT<0 OR MT<=NT OR MT>30 THEN 2600 : REM re-input
2649 REM alter Y scale
2650 CLS : REM clear screen
2655 PRINT
2660 PRINT " Minimum value of ";Y$;" ";
2665 INPUT NY
2670 PRINT
```

```
2675 PRINT " Maximum value of ";Y$;" ";
2680 INPUT MY
2700 GOTO 2030 : REM re-calculate / re-draw
2790 MODE 7 : REM re-set screen
2800 RETURN
2899 REM subroutine plot text Z$ at (XG,YG)
2900 VDU 5
2905 MOVE XG,YG
2910 GCOL 0,0 : REM black
2915 PRINT Z$
2920 VDU 4
2925 RETURN
```

Index

Butterworths BASIC Books

The Butterworths BASIC Books series is the first coherent series to link undergraduate studies with computer programming using the language BASIC – the simplest of all computer languages and the one which is spoken by virtually all micros. Each book demonstrates how computing methods can be used to solve real problems in its subject area, and the series as a whole is the first to promote the computer as a learning tool. Each book contains tested and practical computer programs but also encourages readers to develop their own programming. The books are suitable for undergraduates and practising engineers.

The series covers topics in:

Civil Engineering

Mechanical and Aeronautical Engineering

Mathematics and Statistics

Materials and Metallurgy

Full details of all titles in the series are available from

Butterworths
Borough Green, Sevenoaks, Kent TN15 8PH

BASIC Software

Discs (5¼ in.) and cassettes of programmes in this book
are available for various micros, including:

Apple
BBC Model B
Research Machines 3802 and 4802
Sinclair Spectrum

Write to the publishers for details:

BASIC Books,
Butterworth Scientific Ltd,
PO Box 63
Westbury House,
Bury Street,
Guildford,
SURREY GU2 5BH